Collins

Cambridge IGCSE™

Chemistry

REVISION GUIDE

Chris Sunley

About this Revision book

REVISE

These pages provide a recap of everything you need to know for each topic and include key points to focus on and **key terms** to be learned (full definitions are given in the Glossary). Supplementary content, for the Extended papers, is clearly marked with **S**.

You should read through all the information before taking the Quick Test at the end. This will test whether you can recall the key facts.

> **Quick Test**
>
> 1. In which state of matter are the particles furthest apart?
> 2. What is the name of the process in which a gas forms a liquid?
> 3. State two ways of reducing the volume of a gas.
> **S** 4. Use kinetic particle theory to explain what happens to the particles in a gas when the pressure is increased.
> **S** 5. Water is heated from room temperature to its boiling point and a heating curve is drawn. At what part of the heating curve will the gradient of the curve be the greatest?

PRACTISE

These topic-based exam-style questions appear at the end of a revision section and will test whether you have understood the topic. If you get any of the questions wrong, make sure you read the correct answer carefully.

For selected questions, Show Me features give you guidance on how to structure your answer.

> **Show me**
>
> The atomic structure is $^{16}_{8}O$.
>
> The number of electrons (given by the proton number) = _____
>
> The electron arrangement is _____ so the group number (equal to the number of
>
> electrons in the outer shell) = _____

MIXED QUESTIONS

These pages feature a mix of exam-style questions for all the different topics, just like you would get in an exam. They will make sure you can recall the relevant information to answer a question without being told which topic it relates to.

PRACTICE PAPERS

These pages provide a full set of exam-style practice papers: Paper 1 Multiple Choice (Core)/Paper 2 Multiple Choice (Extended), Paper 3 Theory (Core)/Paper 4 Theory (Extended) and Paper 6 Alternative to Practical. Practise your exam technique in preparation for the Cambridge IGCSE™.

ebook

To access the ebook visit

collins.co.uk/ebooks

and follow the step-by-step instructions.

CONTENTS

Solids, liquids and gases

Learning aims:

Syllabus links:
1.1.1–1.1.4,
S 1.1.5–1.1.6

- Describe the structures of solids, liquids and gases.
- Describe the changes of state.
- Describe the factors that can affect the volume of a gas.
- **S** Explain changes in solids, liquids and gases in terms of kinetic particle theory.

Solids, liquids and gases

In **solids**, the particles are held tightly in a fixed position – so solids have a fixed volume and shape.

In **liquids**, the particles are held together but can move around – so liquids have a fixed volume but no definite shape.

In **gases**, the particles are further apart than in solids and liquids and can move far apart from each other – so gases have no fixed volume or shape.

> **Key Point**
>
> Solids, liquids and gases are called the states of matter.

Changes of state

The processes that involve a **change of state** include:

- **melting** – solid to liquid
- **evaporating** – liquid to gas
- **boiling** – liquid to gas
- **condensing** – gas to liquid
- **freezing** – liquid to solid.

S These processes can be explained using the **kinetic particle theory**:

State of matter	State of matter	Kinetic particle theory
Solid	Liquid	At the melting point the strong forces of attraction holding the particles together in the solid are broken.
Liquid	Gas	During evaporation and at the boiling point the forces of attraction between the particles in the liquid are completely broken. A gas is formed and the particles move randomly.

Increasing the pressure causes the volume of a gas to decrease. Increasing the temperature causes the volume of a gas to increase.

S The changes in volume of a gas can be explained using the kinetic particle theory:

Change made to the gas	Explanation in terms of kinetic particle theory
Increasing pressure	The particles in the gas are forced closer together and the gaps between the particles will be reduced, causing a reduction in volume.
Increasing temperature	The particles in the gas will gain energy and move further apart, causing the volume to increase.

Heating and cooling curves

The kinetic particle theory can also explain **heating curves** and **cooling curves**.

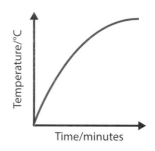 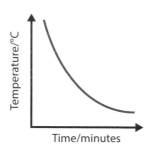

- The gradient of the heating curve decreases as the boiling point is reached. Initially the movement of the particles increases rapidly, but the increase in movement reduces as boiling point is reached.

- The gradient of the cooling curve is greatest as the boiling water starts to cool. Initially the liquid particles lose energy more quickly, but this loss of kinetic energy slows down as room temperature is reached.

Quick Test

1. In which state of matter are the particles furthest apart?
2. What is the name of the process in which a gas forms a liquid?
3. State two ways of reducing the volume of a gas.
   S 4. Use kinetic particle theory to explain what happens to the particles in a gas when the pressure is increased.
   S 5. Water is heated from room temperature to its boiling point and a heating curve is drawn. At what part of the heating curve will the gradient of the curve be the greatest?

Diffusion

Syllabus links:

1.2.1, **S** **1.2.2**

Learning aims:

- Describe and explain diffusion using kinetic particle theory.
- **S** Describe and explain the different speeds of diffusion of gases.

Diffusion

Diffusion is the random mixing and moving of particles in liquids and gases.

The **kinetic particle theory** can be used to explain why the particles in liquids and gases are able to diffuse. The particles in liquids and gases can move and mix.

In liquids, diffusion can be demonstrated by adding coloured crystals to water and watching the dissolving process.

> **Key Point**
>
> Remember that the kinetic particle theory was used in solids, liquids and gases to explain changes of state, for example solid to liquid or liquid to gas.

> **Key Point**
>
> The particles of the crystal spread in the water even if the water is left absolutely still (without any stirring).

When gases mix, the particles of the gases move to fill the space they are in. In the diagrams below, the rapid movement of the molecules in the air and hydrogen means that the particles will diffuse and mix.

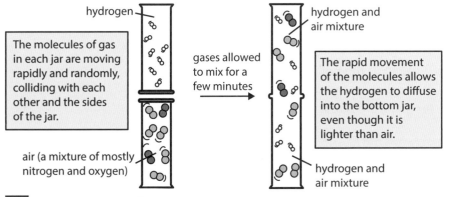

hydrogen

The molecules of gas in each jar are moving rapidly and randomly, colliding with each other and the sides of the jar.

air (a mixture of mostly nitrogen and oxygen)

gases allowed to mix for a few minutes

hydrogen and air mixture

The rapid movement of the molecules allows the hydrogen to diffuse into the bottom jar, even though it is lighter than air.

hydrogen and air mixture

S Speed of diffusion

Gases with different **relative molecular masses** will diffuse at different speeds.

The lower the relative molecular mass of a gas, the greater its rate of diffusion. So, for example, hydrogen with a relative molecular mass of 2 will be the gas that diffuses most rapidly of any gas.

> **Key Point**
>
> A relative molecular mass of a gas can be calculated from the relative atomic masses of the atoms making up the molecule of the gas. For example, H_2 has a relative molecular mass of $1 + 1 = 2$; O_2 has a relative molecular mass of $16 + 16 = 32$. You will learn more about this in Section 3.

Practical skills

The different diffusion rates of gases can be demonstrated in a simple experiment like the one shown below.

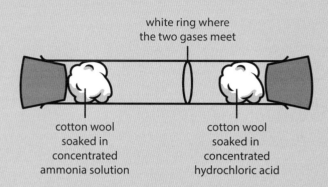

white ring where the two gases meet

cotton wool soaked in concentrated ammonia solution

cotton wool soaked in concentrated hydrochloric acid

The ammonia gas reacts with the hydrogen chloride gas to form a white ring. The position of the ring shows the distance travelled by each gas. As the relative molecular mass of ammonia (17) is less than half the relative molecular mass of the hydrogen chloride (36.5), the ammonia gas will diffuse more quickly than the hydrogen chloride, actually just over twice as quickly. (36.5/17 = 2.15)

Key Point

Concentrated ammonia solution releases the gas ammonia. Concentrated hydrochloric acid releases the gas hydrogen chloride.

Key Point

In the examination you could be asked to explain what precautions you would need to take in setting up this experiment.

Quick Test

1. What is diffusion?
2. In which states of matter does diffusion take place?
S 3. What is the relative molecular mass of carbon dioxide, CO_2?
   (Relative atomic masses: A_r, C = 12, O = 16)
S 4. Which of the following gases will diffuse the most rapidly?
   Nitrogen, N_2; chlorine, Cl_2; methane CH_4
   (Relative atomic masses: A_r H = 1, C = 12, N = 14, Cl = 35.5)

Atomic structure and the Periodic Table

Syllabus links:
2.1.1, 2.2.1–2.2.6

Learning aims:

- Describe the terms elements, compounds and mixtures.

- Describe the structure of an atom.

- Determine the electron configuration of atoms and ions.

- Explain how the position of an element in the Periodic Table can be used to work out its electron arrangement.

Elements, compounds and mixtures

An **element** is the smallest part of a substance that can exist in its own, for example hydrogen or iron.

A **compound** is formed when two or more elements combine chemically, for example water, which is a combination of hydrogen and oxygen.

A **mixture** contains at least two components that are not combined chemically and so can be separated easily, for example sand and salt (salt dissolves in water; sand does not).

Atomic structure

Elements are made up of **atoms**. Atoms are made up of the sub-atomic particles **protons**, **neutrons** and **electrons**.

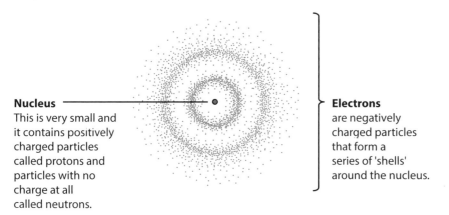

Nucleus
This is very small and it contains positively charged particles called protons and particles with no charge at all called neutrons.

Electrons
are negatively charged particles that form a series of 'shells' around the nucleus.

> **Key Point**

The number of electrons in an atom is equal to the number of protons, so their charges cancel each other out – atoms have no charge.

The relative masses and charges of the sub-atomic particles are shown in the table.

Sub-atomic particle	Relative mass	Relative charge
Proton	1	+1
Neutron	1	0
Electron	about $\frac{1}{2000}$	−1

The **nucleus** has a positive charge as it contains the positively charged protons. The **electron shells** have a negative charge as the electrons have a negative charge.

The **proton number** (or **atomic number**) gives the number of protons in the nucleus; the **mass number** (or **nucleon number**) gives the total number of protons and neutrons in the nucleus.

The diagram shows the sub-atomic particles in an atom.

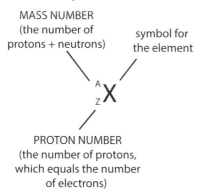

The electron shells hold different numbers of electrons. The first shell can hold just two electrons. The second and third shells can hold up to eight electrons each. For example, a sodium atom has 11 protons in the nucleus and 11 electrons arranged 2,8,1 in shells.

Element	H	He	Li	Be	B	C	N	O	F	Ne
Electron arrangement	1	2	2,1	2,2	2,3	2,4	2,5	2,6	2,7	2,8

The atomic structure of an atom can be shown with an atom diagram.

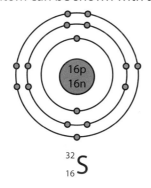

$^{32}_{16}S$

> **Key Point**
>
> The chemical properties of an element depend on the number of electrons in its outer electron shell. Therefore, elements in the same group will have similar chemical properties.

The Periodic Table

The **Periodic Table** shows how atoms are arranged. The elements are arranged in order of proton number.

- The vertical columns are called **groups** and the rows are called **periods**.
- There are eight groups in the Periodic Table labelled I to VIII.
- From Groups I to VII, the atoms of elements in a particular group all have the same number of electrons in their outer electron shell.
- Atoms of all Group VIII elements have a full outer shell of electrons.
- The number of occupied electron shells is equal to the period number. For example, aluminium has three occupied electron shells, arranged as 2,8,3, so is in the 3rd period.

> **Key Point**
>
> Remember you can work out the group number from the number of electrons in the outer electron shell of the atom.

> **Quick Test**
>
> 1. Explain why clean air is not a compound.
> 2. What is the relative charge of a neutron?
> 3. The atomic structure of a carbon atom can be represented by $^{12}_{6}C$.
>   a) What is the mass/nucleon number of this carbon atom?
>   b) Draw an atom diagram for this carbon atom.
>   c) Use your atom diagram to explain why carbon must be in Group IV of the Periodic Table.
>   d) What is the period number for the carbon atom?

Isotopes

Learning aims:

Syllabus links:

2.3.1–2.3.2, **S** 2.3.3–2.3.4

- Know the similarities and differences between isotopes of the same element.

- Use symbols for isotopes and their ions using the proton/atomic number and mass/nucleon number.

- **S** Calculate the relative atomic mass of an element that has two or more main isotopes.

- **S** Explain why isotopes of the same element have the same chemical properties.

Atoms

Atom symbols in the Periodic Table show the proton/atomic number and the mass/nucleon number. So, for example, $_3^7Li$, for the lithium atom.

The same system can be used for **ions**. The electron configuration of lithium is 2,1 (Group I) and so the lithium ion is Li^+ (the electron in the outer shell has been transferred). As the numbers of protons and neutrons have not changed, the lithium ion can be represented by $_3^7Li^+$.

> **Key Point**
>
> A more detailed study of ions is part of Ions and ionic bonds on page 14.

Isotopes

An **isotope** is an atom of an element that has the same number of protons and electrons but different numbers of neutrons to another atom of the same element. For example, hydrogen has an isotope called deuterium. The numbers of sub-atomic particles in these two isotopes are shown in the table.

Isotope	Number of protons	Number of electrons	Number of neutrons
Hydrogen, H	1	1	1
Deuterium, H	1	1	2

The symbols for these two isotopes are hydrogen, $_1^1H$, and deuterium, $_1^2H$.

S Where atoms have more than one isotope, the abundances of the different isotopes can affect the **relative atomic mass** of the atom. For example, the relative atomic mass of chlorine, Cl, is 35.5, which cannot be its **mass/nucleon number** as this must be a whole number.

The table shows two isotopes of boron and their abundances. The calculation shows how the relative atomic mass of boron can be calculated.

Symbol	Abundance (%)
$^{10}_{5}B$	20
$^{11}_{5}B$	80

The relative atomic mass of

$$boron = \frac{(10 \times 20) + (11 \times 80)}{100}$$

$$= \frac{200 + 880}{100}$$

$$= 10.8$$

Isotopes of the same element will have the same chemical properties as they have the same number of electrons and the same electron configurations.

> **Key Point**
>
> If you are asked to do a calculation like this in an examination, it is important to show very clearly the different steps in your calculation. Doing this may help you gain the marks for each section of the calculation. You could get most of the marks even if the final answer is wrong!

> **Quick Test**
>
> 1. What is an isotope?
> 2. The symbol for the potassium atom is $^{39}_{19}K$. Complete the table below for the potassium atom.
>
> | Symbol | Number of protons | Number of electrons | Number of neutrons |
> |---|---|---|---|
> | $^{39}_{19}K$ | | | |
>
> 3. The symbol for the oxygen ion (oxide ion) is $^{16}_{8}O^{2-}$.
>   a) How many protons and neutrons are there in the ion?
>   b) How many electrons are in the ion and what is the electron configuration?
> S 4. Why do isotopes of the same element have the same chemical properties?
> S 5. To calculate the relative atomic mass of an element that has two isotopes, what information is needed in addition to the proton and mass numbers?

> **Key Point**
>
> The term electron configuration is often used in examinations and means electron arrangement.

Ions and ionic bonds

Learning aims:

* Describe the formation of ions.
* Describe the formation of ionic bonds using dot-and-cross diagrams.
* S Describe the giant ionic structure of ionic compounds.
* S Explain the properties of ionic compounds.

Syllabus links:

2.4.1–2.4.4, S 2.4.5–2.4.7

Ions

Ions are formed when atoms lose or gain electrons.

* When an atom loses an electron it forms a positive ion, called a **cation**.
* When an atom gains an electron it forms a negative ion, called an **anion**.

> **Key Point**
>
> Anions and cations have full outer electron shells.

Ionic bonds

Metals lose electrons and non-metals gain electrons when forming ionic bonds. A metal in Group I of the Periodic Table will lose one electron and a non-metal in group VII will gain one electron.

An ionic bond is a strong electrostatic attraction between oppositely charged ions.

When an ionic bond forms between atoms in Group I and Group VII, the cation will have a charge of 1+ and the anion a charge of 1−. An example is shown below in a **dot-and-cross diagram**: one electron is transferred from the sodium atom to the chlorine atom, forming the Na^+ and Cl^- ions.

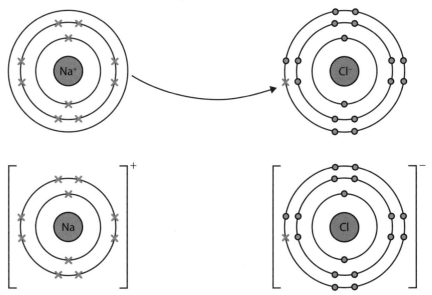

S The dot-and-cross diagram below shows how the ionic compound magnesium oxide is formed containing Mg^{2+} and O^{2-} ions.

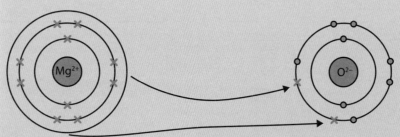

Properties of ionic compounds

The properties of ionic compounds include:

- high melting and boiling points
- good electrical conductivity when molten or when dissolved in water
- poor electrical conductivity when solid.

S The properties of ionic compounds are explained in the table.

Property	Explanation
High melting and boiling points	Strong forces of electrostatic attraction between the oppositely charged ions
Conductivity when solid	The ions are unable to move when an electric current is applied because of the strong forces of attraction.
Conductivity when dissolved in water or when molten	The strong forces of attraction between the ions are broken – the ions are free to move and carry an electric current.

The ions in an ionic compound from a **giant lattice structure**. The lattice structure involves a regular arrangement of alternative positive and negative ions, with each ion bonded to six oppositely charged ions.

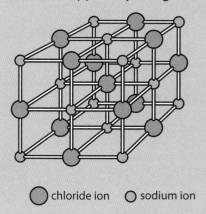

⬤ chloride ion   ◯ sodium ion

Key Point

A giant lattice structure is always a 3D structure.

> **Quick Test**

1. What is a cation?
2. Potassium is in Group I. When the compound potassium chloride is formed:
   a) How many electrons does the potassium atom transfer to the chlorine atom?
   b) What is the charge on the potassium ion that forms?
3. Will calcium chloride have a low or high melting point? Explain your answer.
   S 4. Explain why the formula of the ionic compound aluminium oxide is Al_2O_3.
   S 5. Explain what a giant ionic lattice structure is.

Simple molecules and covalent bonds

Syllabus links:

2.5.1–2.5.3, **S** 2.5.4–2.5.5

Learning aims:

- Describe the nature of a covalent bond.

- Use dot-and-cross diagrams to show single covalent bonding in simple molecules.

- Describe the properties of covalent compounds.

- **S** Use dot-and-cross diagrams to show double and triple covalent bonds.

- **S** Explain the properties of covalent compounds.

Covalent bonds

A single **covalent bond** is formed when a pair of electrons is shared between two atoms.

The sharing of the pair of electrons allows each atom to achieve complete outer electron shells – the noble gas configuration.

A dot-and-cross diagram can be used to show the formation of single covalent bonds, for example in water and methane as shown below.

> **Key Point**
>
> Covalent bonds are formed between non-metals. Ionic bonds are formed between a metal and a non-metal.

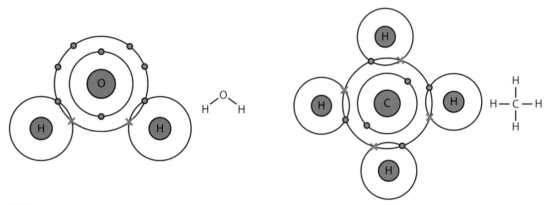

S Double and triple covalent bonds

A double covalent bond is formed by the sharing of four electrons between the two atoms (each atom contributing two electrons).

A dot-and-cross diagram can be used to show the formation of double as well as single bonds, for example the hydrocarbon ethene, as shown below.

> **Key Point**
>
> Ethene is a compound containing just hydrogen and carbon atoms (a hydrocarbon), which is covered as part of Section 11, Organic chemistry.

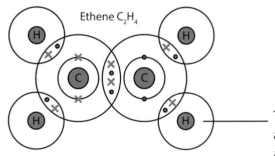

Ethene C_2H_4

Temperatures in a car engine are high and in these conditions, nitrogen in the air can react with oxygen,

A triple covalent bond is formed by the sharing of six electrons between two atoms (each atom contributing three electrons), for example, nitrogen as shown below.

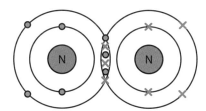

$$N \equiv N$$

Properties of covalent compounds

The properties of covalent compounds include:

- low melting and boiling points
- poor electrical conductivity.

S The properties of covalent compounds are explained in the table.

Property	Explanation
Low melting and boiling points	Weak **intermolecular** forces between the molecules
Poor electrical conductivity	There are no ions or free electrons present to carry the electric current.

> **Key Point**
>
> It is important to be able to explain the differences in properties of ionic and covalent compounds.

> **Quick Test**

1. Define a single covalent bond.
2. Chlorine is a covalent molecule with a formula of Cl_2.
   a) How many electrons does an atom of chlorine have in its outer electron shell?
   b) How many electrons must be shared between the two chlorine atoms?
   c) Draw a dot-and-cross diagram for chlorine, Cl_2.
3. Would you expect hydrogen, H_2, to conduct electricity?
S 4. Explain why ethene has low melting and boiling points.

Giant covalent structures

Learning aims:

- Describe the structures of diamond and graphite.
- Link the structures of diamond and graphite to their uses.
- **S** Describe the structure of silicon(IV) oxide.
- **S** Compare the structures of diamond and silicon(IV) oxide.

Syllabus links:
2.6.1–2.6.2, **S** 2.6.3–2.6.4

Diamond

Diamond has a **giant covalent structure** with each carbon atom strongly covalently bonded to four other atoms, as shown in the diagram.

—— strong bond

Diamond is used in cutting tools as it has such a strong structure and is not easily worn down or broken.

Graphite

Graphite also has a giant covalent structure, but it is very different from that of diamond. Each carbon atom forms three strong covalent bonds to other carbon atoms.

Graphite has a layered structure with weak forces of attraction between the layers, as shown in the diagram.

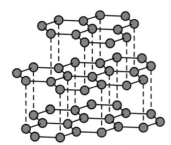

Structure of graphite

In graphite the fourth unbonded electron from each carbon atom is **delocalised** (not in a fixed position) and so can move.

Graphite has two important uses:

- As a **lubricant**. This is because the weak forces of attraction between the layers in the structure means that the layers can slide over each other.
- As an **electrode**. The delocalised electrons that are not used in covalent bonds, one from each carbon atom, will move when the graphite is attached to an electrical circuit.

> **Key Point**
>
> Electrodes are important parts of the electrical circuits used in electrolysis. You should remember that the positive electrode is the **anode** (it attracts anions) and the negative electrode is the **cathode** (it attracts cations).

S Silicon(IV) oxide

Silicon(IV) oxide, SiO_2, also has a giant covalent structure, as shown in the diagram below:

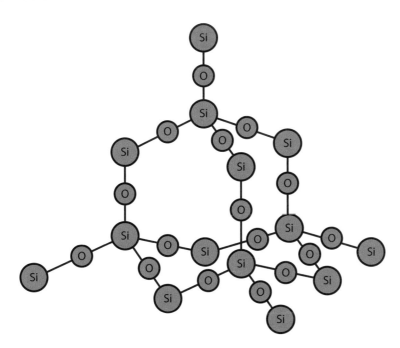

> ### Key Point
>
> Ethene is a compound containing just hydrogen and carbon atoms (a hydrocarbon), which is covered as part of Section 11, Organic chemistry.

The structure of silicon(IV) oxide is similar to that of diamond in that each silicon atom is covalently bonded to four oxygen atoms.

As silicon(IV) oxide and diamond have similar structures, they have similar properties, as shown in the table.

Diamond and silicon(IV) oxide	Explanation
High melting and boiling points	The giant covalent structures are both very strong with carbon and silicon atoms strongly bonded to four other atoms.
No electrical conductivity	They are non-conductors as there are no ions or delocalised electrons in their structures.

> ### Quick Test
>
> 1. How many covalent bonds does each carbon atom form in:
>   a) diamond?
>   b) graphite?
> 2. What part of the structure of graphite means it can act as an electrode?
> S 3. How many covalent bonds are formed by each silicon atom in silicon(IV) oxide?
> S 4. Why is the melting point of diamond so much higher than that of a simple covalent compound such as iodine?

S Metallic bonding

Learning aims:

- S Describe metallic bonding.
- S Explain the properties of metals in terms of their structure and bonding.

Structure of metals

Metals are made up of a giant lattice structure containing metal ions surrounded by a 'sea' of **delocalised electrons**. This is represented by the diagram below.

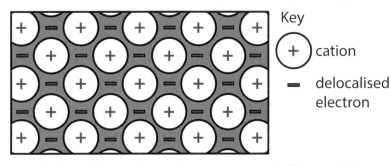

Key
+ cation
− delocalised electron

> **Key Point**
>
> Remember that metals form **cations** (positive ions) by losing electrons from the outer electron shell.

- The term lattice refers to the regular arrangement of the metal ions.
- The term delocalised electrons means electrons that have no fixed position. They are sometimes referred to as a 'sea', because they can move freely.

The negative electrons are attracted to the positive ions and hold the structure together. This attraction is called **electrostatic**.

> **Key Point**
>
> Remember that delocalised electrons also are a key part of the structure of graphite.

Properties of metals

Useful properties of metals include:

- high melting and boiling points (characteristics of all giant structures)
- good electrical conductivity
- **malleable** (can be beaten into sheets) – for example, iron can be used as covers for drains
- **ductile** (can be drawn into wires) – for example, copper can be used for electrical wiring.

The properties of metals and their explanations in terms of structure are given in the table.

Property of a metal	Explanation in terms of structure
Usually a high melting point	Strong electrostatic forces between the ions and the sea of electrons
Usually a high boiling point	Strong electrostatic forces between the ions and the sea of electrons
Good electrical conductivity	Delocalised electrons are able to move freely through the structure.
Malleable (can be beaten into sheets)	Ions can move around into different positions when the metal is hammered
Ductile (can be drawn into wires)	Ions can move into different positions when the metal is stretched.

> **Quick Test**

S **1.** What is a cation?

S **2.** Why can the electrons in a metal structure be referred to as a 'sea'?

S **3.** Give **two** reasons why copper is a suitable element to use in electrical wiring.

S **4.** What does the term malleable mean?

S **5.** Name a giant covalent structure which, like most metals, has high melting and boiling points.

Formulae

Learning aims:

- Write the molecular formulae of elements and compounds, including from models and diagrams.

- Construct word equations and symbol equations including state symbols.

- **S** Use the empirical formula of a compound.

- **S** Use information to write symbol equations, including ionic equations.

Syllabus links: 3.1.1–3.1.4, S 3.1.5–3.1.8

Formulae

An ionic compound can be represented by a **formula**, and a covalent compound by a **molecular formula**.

The formula of a compound can be worked out using the Group number or the combining powers of elements in the Periodic Table. The Group number indicates the number of electrons in the outer electron shell of an atom:

Group Number	I	II	III	IV	V	VI	VII
Number of electrons in the outer electron shell	1	2	3	4	5	6	7
Combining power	1	2	3	4	3	2	1

The formula of a compound can be worked out from models and diagrams (see Figs. 3.1 and 3.2).

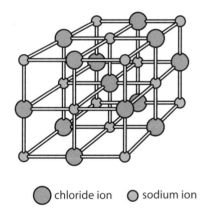

○ chloride ion ○ sodium ion

Fig. 3.1 The model shows the arrangement of ions in sodium chloride. The formula is NaCl

$$H-C-C-H$$

Fig. 3.2 The displayed formula of ethane shows the formula is C_2H_6

> **Key Point**
>
> Elements in Group VIII, the noble gases, generally do not form compounds. In Group VIII the outer electron shells are full (containing either 2 or 8 electrons).

> **Key Point**
>
> Metals lose electrons in forming ionic compounds. Non-metals either gain electrons in forming ionic compounds or share electrons in forming covalent compounds.

S The formula of an ionic compound can be worked out from the charges on the ions present. Examples include:

Ionic compound	Ions present	Formula
Potassium chloride	K^+ and Cl^-	KCl
Calcium carbonate	Ca^{2+} and CO_3^{2-}	$CaCO_3$
Copper(II) sulfate	Cu^{2+} and SO_4^{2-}	$CuSO_4$

An **empirical formula** is the simplest whole number ratio of the different atoms or ions in a compound. Examples include:

Compound	Molecular formula	Empirical formula
Ethane	C_2H_6	CH_3
Butane	C_4H_{10}	C_2H_5
Glucose	$C_6H_{12}O_6$	CH_2O

Equations

Word equations and **symbol equations** are used to represent reactions. The equations can include state symbols: (s) for solid, (l) for liquid, (aq) for aqueous/solution and (g) for gas.

For example, when carbon burns in oxygen to form carbon dioxide, the word and symbol equations are:

$$\text{carbon(s)} + \text{oxygen(g)} \rightarrow \text{carbon dioxide(g)}$$
$$C(s) + O_2(g) \rightarrow CO_2(g)$$

S **Ionic equations** can also be written using state symbols. Examples include:

Reaction	Ionic equation
Copper(II) ions react with hydroxide ions to form copper(II) hydroxide	$Cu^{2+}(aq) + 2OH^-(aq) \rightarrow Cu(OH)_2(s)$
Hydrogen ions react with carbonate ions to produce carbon dioxide and water	$2H^+(aq) + CO_3^{2-}(aq) \rightarrow CO_2(g) + H_2O(l)$

Quick Test

1. What is the formula of magnesium chloride?
2. Sodium reacts with oxygen to form solid sodium oxide.
   Write a balanced symbol equation for the reaction, including state symbols.

S 3. Construct an ionic equation, with state symbols, for the reaction between iron(III) ions and hydroxide ions to form solid iron(III) hydroxide.

Relative masses of atoms and molecules

Learning aims:

- Define relative atomic mass and relative molecular mass.

- Perform calculations involving reacting masses.

Relative atomic mass

Relative atomic mass, A_r, is the average mass of the isotopes of an element compared to 1/12th the mass of an atom of ^{12}C.

The relative atomic mass of an element is usually a whole number but not always, e.g. chlorine has an A_r of 35.5.

Relative molecular mass

Relative molecular mass, M_r, is the sum of the relative atomic masses of the atoms in a molecule of a compound. For example:

A_r C = 12 and H = 1, so the M_r of methane, CH_4, is $12 + 1 + 1 + 1 + 1 = 16$.

Relative formula mass, M_r, is used for ionic compounds (ionic compounds do not have molecules). For example:

A_r Na = 23 and Cl = 35.5, so the M_r of sodium chloride, NaCl, is
$23 + 35.5 = 58.5$.

Reacting masses

Reacting masses can be used with a balanced chemical equation to work out the quantities of reactants and products.

> **Key Point**
>
> Remember that isotopes are atoms of the same element with the same numbers of protons but different numbers of neutrons.

> **Key Point**
>
> You do not need to remember the relative atomic masses of elements. In an examination these will always be provided and included on the copy of the Periodic Table.

> **Key Point**
>
> It is important to follow a particular sequence in reacting masses calculations, as shown in the examples below.

Example 1   8 g of hydrogen is burnt in excess oxygen. What mass of water will be formed? (A_r H = 1, O = 16)

Sequence	Calculation
Write down the balanced equation	$2H_2 + O_2 \rightarrow 2H_2O$
Write down the relative molecular mass / formula mass of each reactant and product	$4 + 32 \rightarrow 36$ $\Downarrow$
Write down the quantity/quantities given in the question and then scale up or down all quantities by the same proportion	$8\,g + 64\,g \rightarrow 72\,g$ (double)

Example 2 When magnesium reacts with excess hydrochloric acid, 1 g of hydrogen is produced. What mass of magnesium is needed to produce this mass of hydrogen? (A_r Mg = 24, H = 1)

Sequence	Calculation
Write down the balanced equation	$Mg(s) + 2HCl(aq) \rightarrow MgCl_2(aq) + H_2(g)$ 24 $\rightarrow$ 2
Write down the relative molecular mass / formula mass of each reactant and product	$\Downarrow$ 12 g $\rightarrow$ 1 g (half)
Write down the quantity/ quantities given in the question and then scale up or down all quantities by the same proportion	

Key Point

Including the state symbols does not affect the calculation.

Example 3 When 64 g of methane (CH_4) is burnt in excess oxygen, what masses of carbon dioxide and water will be produced? (A_r H = 1, C = 12, O = 16)

Sequence	Calculation
Write down the balanced equation	$CH_4(g) + 2O_2(g) \rightarrow CO_2(g) + 2H_2O(l)$ 16 $\rightarrow$ 44 + 36
Write down the relative molecular mass / formula mass of each reactant and product	$\Downarrow$ 64 g $\rightarrow$ 156 g + 144 g
Write down the quantity/ quantities given in the question and then scale up or down all quantities by the same proportion	(multiply by 4)

Key Point

In an examination you may get some marks if you follow the above sequence even if you make a mistake and get the wrong answer.

> **Quick Test**

1. Define the term relative atomic mass.
2. What is the relative molecular mass of glucose, $C_6H_{12}O_6$?
   (A_r H = 1, C = 12, O = 16)
3. What is the relative formula mass of potassium carbonate, K_2CO_3?
   (A_r C = 12, O = 16, K = 39)
4. What mass of carbon dioxide will be produced from burning 36 g of carbon? (A_r C = 12, O = 16)

The mole and the Avogadro constant

Syllabus links:
3.3.1, [S] 3.3.2–3.3.8

Learning aims:

- Know the units for the concentration of solutions.
- [S] Know what the mole is.
- [S] Carry out calculations using the mole concept involving mass, volume and number of particles.
- [S] Calculate empirical and molecular formulae and percentage yield.

The mole and the Avogadro constant

The concentration of a solution is measured in g/dm^3 or mol/dm^3.
($1\ dm^3 = 1000\ cm^3$)

> [S] The **mole**, mol, is the unit of an amount of substance that contains 6.02×10^{23} particles. This number is known as the **Avogadro constant**.
>
> The amount of a substance can be calculated using the following equation:
>
> $$\text{amount of substance (mol)} = \frac{\text{mass (g)}}{\text{molar mass (g/mol)}}$$

> **Example 1** How many moles of carbon are there in 24 g of carbon? (A_r C = 12)
>
> $\text{moles} = \dfrac{24}{12} = 2$

> **Example 2** How many particles are there in 0.5 moles of magnesium?
>
> $\text{number of particles} = 0.5 \times 6.02 \times 10^{23} = 3.01 \times 10^{23}$

[S] Molar gas volume

The **molar gas volume** (the volume occupied by 1 mole of a gas) is $24\ dm^3$ at room temperature and pressure (r.t.p.).

[S] Reaction equations

> **Example 3** What mass of potassium oxide is formed when 39 g of potassium is burnt in excess oxygen? (A_r O = 16, K = 39)

Sequence	Calculation
Write down the balanced equation	$4\,K + O_2 \rightarrow 2\,K_2O$
Write down the number of moles of each component of the equation	$4\ mol + 1\ mol \rightarrow 2\ mol$ $156\ g \qquad\qquad \rightarrow 94\ g$
Convert the number of moles to the unit given in the question, e.g. mass (g) or volume (dm^3)	$\Downarrow$ $39\ g \qquad\qquad \rightarrow 23.5\ g$ (divide by 4)
Write down the quantity/quantities given in the question and then scale up or down all quantities by the same proportion	

> **Key Point**
>
> This topic will involve you in doing calculations. Remember you must always show your working as you can score marks for the working.

> **Key Point**
>
> As used with calculations in the previous topic, it is helpful to follow a sequence.

S Percentage yield

In experiments like the one above, the amount of potassium oxide formed may be less than predicted from the equation. The amount actually produced can be used to calculate the **percentage yield**. For example, if 20.0 g of K_2O is produced then:

$$\text{percentage yield} = \frac{20.0}{23.5} \times 100 = 85\%$$

S Titrations

Titration calculations can be performed using the mole concept.

> **Key Point**
>
> You will do further work on titrations in Section 12 on pages 118–121.

Example 4 25 dm³ of 0.1M sodium hydroxide solution reacts with 12.5 dm³ of hydrochloric acid solution in a titration. Calculate the concentration of the hydrochloric acid. (M stands for moles/dm³)

Sequence	Calculation
Write down the balanced equation	$HCl + NaOH \rightarrow NaCl + H_2O$
Write down the number of moles of each component of the equation	1 mol + 1 mol → 1 mol + 1 mol 1000 cm³ 1000 cm³
Convert the number of moles to the unit given in the question	0.1M 0.1M 12.5 cm³?M 25 cm³ 0.1M
Write down the quantity/quantities given in the question and then scale up or down all quantities by the same proportion	$\Downarrow$ 0.2M (double the concentration)

S Calculations of empirical and molecular formulae

Example 5 2.3 g of sodium react with 0.8 g of oxygen to form sodium oxide. (A_r O = 16, Na = 23)

$\frac{2.3}{23} = 0.1$ mole Na, $\frac{0.8}{16} = 0.05$ mole O

Ratio is 2:1, so Na_2O is the empirical formula.

> **Quick Test**
>
> S 1. Molar gas volume is always quoted at r.t.p. What does this stand for?
>
> S 2. How many moles are there in 6 g of carbon? (A_r C = 12)
>
> S 3. How many moles are there in 6 dm³ of nitrogen gas?
>
> S 4. How many molecules are there in 32 g of methane, CH_4? (A_r H = 1, C = 12)
>
> S 5. In an experiment 6 dm³ of gas at r.t.p. was expected. However, the percentage yield was only 25%. What volume of gas was collected?

Solids, liquids and gases

1 Identify which of the following is the best description of a liquid.

    A. The particles are held tightly in a fixed position.

    B. The particles are held together but are able to move around.

    C. The particles can only vibrate about a fixed position

    D. The particles have no fixed volume or shape. [1]

'Identify' means you have to select your answer.

2 Identify which of the following describes the change of state in the process of evaporation.

    A. Gas to liquid

    B. Liquid to gas

    C. Liquid to solid

    D. Solid to liquid [1]

3 Describe the effect on the volume of a gas of each of the following:

a Increasing temperature. [1]

b Reducing pressure. [1]

[Total marks 2]

'Describe' means give the main features.

S 4 Sketch a heating curve showing how the temperature of water changes in a kettle as it is heated. You can assume the water has a temperature of 20°C before heating and boils at 100°C. [3]

'Sketch' means make a freehand drawing showing the key features, taking care over proportions. Include labels.

S 5 Use the kinetic particle theory to explain the changes that occur:

a when a liquid turns into a gas. [2]

b when the pressure of a gas is reduced. [2]

[Total marks 4]

Diffusion

1 When blue crystals of copper(II) sulfate are added to water in a beaker, the blue colour starts to spread throughout the water. Use the kinetic particle theory to explain the diffusion that occurs. [2]

'Explain' means set out the reasons for what happens.

2

air —

bromine gas —

The experiment has been set up to show the diffusion of bromine gas when mixed with air. Bromine molecules are much heavier than the molecules in air. The gas jar containing air is placed on top of the gas jar containing bromine. The lids of the gas jars are then removed.

a Bromine is a very toxic gas. Suggest what precautions you would take in setting up this experiment. [2]

'Suggest' means apply your knowledge and understanding to the situation.

b Use kinetic particle theory to describe and explain what happens when the gas jars are left connected for several hours. [2]

'Describe' means give the main features.

c Suggest why the lower gas jar remains more red-brown than the upper gas jar, even when the diffusion is complete. [2]

[Total marks 6]

3 This question is about four gases: hydrogen, H_2, oxygen, O_2, carbon dioxide, CO_2, and chlorine, Cl_2.

The relative atomic masses of the atoms are: $H = 1$, $C = 12$, $O = 16$, $Cl = 35.5$.

a Calculate the relative molecular mass of each gas.

   i) Hydrogen [1]

   ii) Oxygen [1]

   iii) Carbon dioxide [1]

   iv) Chlorine [1]

'Calculate' means work out from the figures given.

b Which of these gases will diffuse most rapidly?

Explain your answer. [2]

c Which of these gases will diffuse least rapidly?

Explain your answer. [2]

[Total marks 8]

Atomic structure and the Periodic Table

1 Identify the correct definition of a compound.

    A. A combination of two or more elements that are mixed

    B. The smallest part of a substance

    C. Two or more elements combined chemically

    D. Two or more elements combined so that they are separated easily   **[1]**

> 'Identify' means you have to select the answer from those provided.

2 Which of the following statements is correct?

    A. In an atom, the numbers of electrons and neutrons are always the same.

    B. In an atom, the numbers of protons and electrons are always the same.

    C. The nucleus always contains equal numbers of protons and neutrons.

    D. The nucleon number gives the number of neutrons in an atom.   **[1]**

3 The symbol for a sodium atom is $^{23}_{11}Na$. Identify the correct atomic structure for sodium.

    A. 11 electrons, 11 neutrons and 12 protons

    B. 11 electrons, 12 neutrons and 11 protons

    C. 12 electrons, 12 neutrons and 11 protons

    D. 23 electrons and protons, and 11 neutrons   **[1]**

4 The atomic structure of the oxygen atom is $^{16}_{8}O$.

a State the number of electrons in the atom.   **[1]**

> 'State' means you must answer the question very precisely. In this question the answer is a number.

b State the electron configuration in the atom.   **[1]**

c Which group of the Periodic Table contains oxygen? Explain how you have deduced this from the atomic structure.   **[2]**

> 'Deduce' means you base your answer on the information given.

> **Show me**
>
> The atomic structure is $^{16}_{8}O$.
>
> The number of electrons (given by the proton number) = ...
>
> The electron arrangement is .... so the group number (equal to the number of
>
> electrons in the outer shell) = ...

d   Sketch an atom diagram for the oxygen atom.   [2]

'Sketch' means make a simple freehand drawing showing the key features – it must be clear but not a work of art.

[Total marks 6]

5   The potassium atom can form an ion. The potassium atom has an atomic structure that can be written as $^{39}_{19}K$.

a   What is the atomic structure of the potassium atom?   [1]

b   What is the atomic structure of the potassium ion?   [1]

[Total marks 2]

Isotopes

1   Which definition of isotopes is correct?

     A. Different atoms of the same element with the same number of neutrons but different numbers of electrons

     B. Different atoms of the same element with the same number of neutrons but different numbers of protons

     C. Different atoms of the same element with the same number of protons but different numbers of electrons

     D. Different atoms of the same element with the same number of protons but different numbers of neutrons   [1]

2   Which row gives the correct atomic structure for the chloride ion, $^{35}_{17}Cl^-$?

	Number of protons	Number of electrons	Number of neutrons
A	17	17	19
B	18	18	17
C	17	18	18
D	17	17	18

[1]

3   Gallium is an element in Group III of the Periodic Table. The two isotopes of gallium are shown in the table.

Isotopes	Number of protons	Number of neutrons	Number of electrons	Relative abundance (%)
$^{69}_{31}Ga$				60
$^{71}_{31}Ga$				40

a   Complete the columns in the table.   [2]

b Explain why the two isotopes of gallium have the same chemical properties. [2]

'Explain' means you must give the reason(s).

c Gallium is in Group III of the Periodic Table. What does this tell you about the electron configuration of gallium? [1]

d Calculate the relative atomic mass of gallium to three significant figures from the relative masses and abundances of its isotopes. [3]

'Calculate' means you have to use the numbers in the table to work out the answer.

> **Show me**

The relative atomic mass of gallium $= \dfrac{(69 \times 60) + (71 \times \quad)}{100}$

$= \dfrac{4140 +}{100} = \text{...}$

$= \text{...}$ (to 3 significant figures)

In calculation questions like this you must show your working. Even if you make a mistake, you may still be awarded some marks.

[Total marks 8]

Ions and ionic bonds

1 Which of the following statements is correct?

   A. A negative ion is called a cation.

   B. A positive ion is called an anion.

   C. An ionic bond is a strong attraction between oppositely charged ions.

   D. An ionic bond is formed when electrons are shared between atoms. [1]

2 Bromine is in Group VII of the Periodic Table. Select the correct answer.

   A. Bromine forms the ion, Br^{7-}.

   B. Bromine forms the ion, Br^{-}.

   C. Bromine forms the ion, Br^{+}.

   D. Bromine does not form an ion. [1]

3 Aluminium has an atomic number of 13. Select the ion that aluminium forms.

   A. Al^{+}

   B. Al^{2+}

   C. Al^{3+}

   D. Al^{4+} [1]

4 Draw a dot and-cross diagram for sodium fluoride, showing how the ions combine.

a Use the atomic numbers to work out the electron arrangements of sodium and fluorine.

Element	Atomic number	Electron arrangement
Sodium	11	
Fluorine	9	

[1]

[1]

b Deduce the formula of sodium fluoride.

Use the electron arrangement: both ions should have complete outer electron shells.	Formula =
	....

[1]

c Sketch a dot-and-cross diagram for each atom.

Show the nucleus as a circle and then the electron shells around the nucleus. Use dots or crosses to show the position of the electrons in the shells.	**Dot-and-cross diagram**
	Sodium
	Fluorine

[1]

[1]

'Sketch' means make a simple freehand drawing showing the key features.

d Draw a dot and cross diagram for sodium fluoride showing how the ions combine.

Combine your diagrams from above to show how the electron transfer takes place.	

[2]

[Total marks 7]

S **5** Aluminium reacts with oxygen to form aluminium oxide.

a Use the Periodic Table on page 179 to complete the table below.

Element	Atomic number	Electron arrangement
Aluminium			[2]
Oxygen			[2]

b Sketch a dot-and-cross diagram to show the formation of the ionic bond between aluminium and oxygen. [2]

c Complete the table below by predicting and explaining the properties of aluminium oxide. You can use terms for your predictions such as: high, low, good, poor.

Property	Prediction/explanation
Melting point		[2]
Boiling point		[2]
Electrical conductivity		[2]

[Total marks 12]

S **6** Describe the features of a giant ionic lattice structure. [2]

Simple molecules and covalent bonds

1 State which of the following elements will **not** form a covalent bond.

A. Carbon

B. Fluorine

C. Hydrogen

D. Potassium [1]

2 State which of the following electron configurations is that of a noble gas.

A. 2,1

B. 2,2

C. 2,6

D. 2,8 [1]

3 Draw a dot-and-cross diagram for hydrogen chloride showing how the atoms combine.

a Use the atomic numbers to work out the electron arrangements of hydrogen and chlorine.

Element	Atomic number	Electron arrangement
Hydrogen	1	
Chlorine	17	

[1]

[1]

b Deduce the formula of hydrogen chloride.

Use the electron arrangement – both atoms should have complete outer electron shells when combined.	Formula =

[1]

c Sketch a dot-and-cross diagram for each atom.

Show the nucleus as a circle and then the electron shells around the nucleus. Use dots or crosses to show the position of the electrons in the shells.	**Dot-and-cross diagram** Hydrogen
	Chlorine

[1]

[1]

'Sketch' means make a simple freehand drawing showing the key features.

d Sketch a dot-and-cross diagram for hydrogen chloride.

Combine your diagrams from above to show how the electron sharing takes place.	

[2]

[Total marks 7]

S 4 a Draw a dot-and-cross diagram to show the covalent bonding in oxygen, O_2. The atomic number of oxygen is 8. [2]

b Complete the table below by predicting and explaining the properties of oxygen. You can use for your predictions terms such as: high, low, good, poor.

Property	Prediction/ explanation	
Melting point		[2]
Boiling point		[2]
Electrical conductivity		[2]

[Total marks 8]

S 5 Sketch a dot-and-cross diagram for ethane, C_2H_6. [3]

Giant covalent structures

1 Which of the following statements is **not** true about graphite?

A. It has a high melting point.

B. It is a form of carbon.

C. It is used as an electrode in electrolysis experiments.

D. It is used in cutting tools. [1]

2 a Sketch and label a diagram that represents the giant structure of diamond. [2]

'Sketch' means make a freehand drawing showing the main features.

b Compare the sketch of the giant structure of diamond you have drawn with the giant structure of graphite. [2]

[Total marks 4]

'Compare' means identify similarities and differences.

S 3 The diagram below shows the giant structure of silicon(**IV**) oxide.

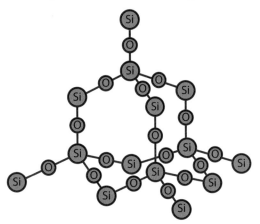

a Explain why the properties of silicon(**IV**) oxide and diamond are similar. [2]

'Explain' means set out the reasons.

b How would you expect the properties of silicon(**IV**) oxide to compare to sodium chloride, which has a giant ionic structure? [3]

[Total marks 5]

s Metallic bonding

1 Explain in terms of structure and bonding each of the following properties of metals:

a Metals have good electrical conductivity. [2]

b Metals usually have high melting points. [2]

c Metals have good ductility. [2]

[Total marks 6]

2 Analyse the information in the table. Use the information to deduce the answers to the questions that follow.

Substance	Melting point (°C)	Electrical conductivity	
		When solid	When molten
A	1085	Good	Good
B	−114	Poor	Poor
C	3550	Poor	Poor
D	801	Poor	Good

a Which of the substances could be copper? [1]

b Which of the substances contains ionic bonds? [1]

c Which of the substances is a simple covalent compound? [1]

d Which of the substances could have a giant covalent structure? [1]

[Total marks 4]

'Analyse' means identify the factors and the relationships between them.

'Deduce' means use the information to arrive at the answer.

3 **a** Sketch and label a diagram that shows part of the giant structure of a metal. [2]

b Describe the features of the giant structure of a metal that explain its electrical conductivity. [2]

'Describe' means give the main features.

c Describe the features of the giant structure of a metal that explain its malleability. [2]

[Total marks 6]

Formulae

1 State the formula of calcium fluoride.

    A. CaF

    B. CaF_2

    C. CaF_3

    D. Ca_2F **[1]**

2 Deduce the molecular formula of butane from the displayed formula below:

$$H-\overset{\displaystyle H}{\underset{\displaystyle H}{C}}-\overset{\displaystyle H}{\underset{\displaystyle H}{C}}-\overset{\displaystyle H}{\underset{\displaystyle H}{C}}-\overset{\displaystyle H}{\underset{\displaystyle H}{C}}-H$$

    A. CH_2

    B. C_2H_5

    C. C_4H_{10}

    D. C_4H_{12} **[1]**

3 Magnesium burns in air to form magnesium oxide.

  a Write a word equation, including state symbols, for this reaction.   **[1]**

  b Write a balanced symbol equation for this reaction.   **[2]**

                                 [Total marks 3]

S 4 State the empirical formula of propene, which has a molecular formula of C_3H_6.

    A. CH

    B. CH_2

    C. C_4H_4

    D. C_3H_6 **[1]**

S 5 Aluminium fluoride is an ionic compound containing Al^{3+} ions and F^- ions. Deduce the formula of aluminium fluoride.   **[1]**

> 'Deduce' means use the information provided.

S 6 Calcium reacts with water to form calcium hydroxide and hydrogen.

  a Write a symbol equation, including state symbols, for this reaction.   **[2]**

  b Write an ionic equation for this reaction.   **[2]**

                                 [Total marks 4]

S 7 Magnesium reacts with copper(II) sulfate as shown in the equation below:

$$Mg(s) + CuSO_4(aq) \rightarrow MgSO_4(aq) + Cu(s)$$

Write an ionic equation for this reaction.   **[2]**

Relative masses of atoms and molecules

1   **a**   The relative atomic mass of an element is compared to the mass of which atom? [1]

  b   Suggest why the relative atomic mass of chlorine, 35.5, is not a whole number. [1]

[Total marks 2]

'Suggest' means apply your knowledge and understanding to provide a reasonable answer.

2   Use the relative atomic masses provided to work out the relative molecular/formula masses of the following compounds.

  a   MgO (A_r O = 16, Mg = 24) [1]

  b Al_2O_3 (A_r O = 16, Al = 27) [1]

  c C_2H_5OH (A_r H = 1, C = 12, O = 16) [1]

  d SiO_2 (A_r O = 16, Si = 28) [1]

[Total marks 4]

3   Hydrogen burns in oxygen to form water as shown in the equation:

$$2H_2(g) + O_2(g) \rightarrow 2H_2O(l)$$

2 g of hydrogen is burnt in excess oxygen. (A_r H = 1, O = 16)

  a   Calculate the mass of oxygen needed to react completely with the hydrogen. [2]

  b   What mass of water will be produced? [2]

> **Show me**

Equation	$2H_2 + O_2 \rightarrow 2H_2O$
Add relative masses	4 +
Add quantity from question	2 g + g g

[Total marks 4]

4   Propane gas (C_3H_8) burns in air to form carbon dioxide and water.

  a   Write a balanced equation for this reaction. [2]

  b   If 22 g of propane (C_3H_8) is burnt, calculate the mass of carbon dioxide that will be produced. (A_r H = 1, C = 12, O = 16) [2]

[Total marks 4]

5 In the blast furnace used for making iron, iron(III) oxide reacts with carbon monoxide to form iron and carbon dioxide. (A_r C = 12, C = 16, Fe = 56)

Write a balanced equation for this reaction. [2]

a If 1.0 kg of iron(III) oxide is converted:

i) calculate the mass of iron that would be produced. [3]

ii) calculate the mass of carbon dioxide that would be produced. [3]

[Total marks 8]

The mole and the Avogadro constant

1 A bottle of hydrochloric acid is labelled 0.1 mol/dm³. Explain what the unit mol/dm³ means. [1]

S 2 State the mass of 0.5 mol of carbon. (Use the Periodic Table on page 179 to determine the relative atomic mass of carbon.)

A. 0.5 g

B. 3 g

C. 6 g

D. 12 g [1]

S 3 Calculate the relative molecular mass of a substance if 0.25 mol has mass 16 g.

A. 8

B. 16

C. 32

D. 64 [1]

S 4 State what mass of water will contain 3.01×10^{22} molecules. (A_r H = 1, O = 16) [3]

> **Show me**

Number of particles	Mass of water (H_2O)	
6.02×10^{23}	1 mole =	g
6.02×10^{22}		g
3.01×10^{22}		g

S 5 In a reaction, 39 g of potassium reacted with 8 g of oxygen to form potassium oxide. Calculate the empirical formula of potassium oxide. (A_r O = 16, K = 39) [2]

6 Calcium reacts with oxygen, forming calcium oxide. (Use the Periodic Table on page 179 for the relative atomic masses you need.)

a Write a fully balanced equation for this reaction. [2]

b An amount of calcium was chosen to produce 7 g of calcium oxide. Calculate the mass of calcium that was chosen. [2]

c In fact, only 5 g of calcium oxide was collected. Calculate the percentage yield in the reaction. [2]

[Total marks 6]

7 Calcium carbonate reacts with dilute hydrochloric acid to produce carbon dioxide. In an experiment 0.2 g of calcium carbonate reacted with excess dilute hydrochloric acid. (Use the Periodic Table on page 179 for the relative atomic masses you need.)

a Sketch and label the apparatus that could be used in this reaction to measure the volume of carbon dioxide used. [2]

'Sketch' means make a simple freehand drawing showing the key features.

b Write down a fully balanced equation for the reaction, including state symbols. [2]

c Calculate the volume of carbon dioxide, measured at room temperature and pressure, which would be produced in the reaction. [3]

[Total marks 7]

8 You have been asked to perform a titration to determine the concentration of a solution of sodium hydroxide. You use a solution of 0.1M hydrochloric acid.

a Sketch and label the apparatus you would use to add the hydrochloric acid to 25 cm^3 of sodium hydroxide solution containing an indicator. [2]

b Write a fully balanced equation for the reaction. [2]

c After performing the titration three times, the volume of hydrochloric acid used was determined to be 20.0 cm^3.

i) Suggest why the titration was performed three times. [1]

ii) Calculate the concentration of the sodium hydroxide solution. [3]

[Total marks 8]

Electrolysis and hydrogen–oxygen fuel cells

Syllabus links:
4.1.1–4.1.7,
S **4.1.8–4.1.11,**
4.2.1, S **4.2.2**

Learning aims:

- Define electrolysis.
- Identify the products formed in the electrolysis of compounds.
- Explain how metal objects are electroplated and the reasons for doing this.
- S Explain the process of electrolysis and use ionic equations.
- Describe a hydrogen–oxygen fuel cell.
- S Describe the advantages the advantages of hydrogen-oxygen fuel cells.

Electrolysis

Electrolysis is the decomposition of an ionic compound, when molten or in aqueous solution, by the passage of an electric current.

> **Key Point**

You may need to revise your knowledge of ions and ionic bonding covered on pages 14–15. The ions need to be able to move so the compound must be molten or in aqueous solution.

> **Practical skills**

To investigate the electrolysis of an aqueous solution you will need to set up an electrical circuit as shown in Fig. 4.1.

Fig. 4.1 A typical electrical circuit used in electrolysis.

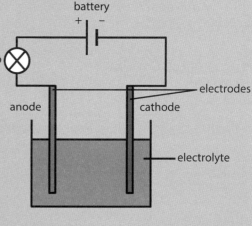

1. You can use a battery or power pack (a direct current must be used).
2. The compound you are testing is called the **electrolyte**.
3. Two electrodes are needed. Carbon/graphite rods can be used as they will not react during the electrolysis. (Platinum can also be used.)
4. One electrode must be attached to the positive terminal of the battery or power supply. This electrode is called the anode. The other electrode must be attached to the negative terminal of the battery or power supply. This electrode is called the cathode.
5. The electrodes must be kept separate from each other – if they touch you will have a short circuit (the electricity will not pass through the electrolyte).
6. You must include either a bulb or an ammeter in the circuit to show whether the circuit is working.

S During the electrolysis, electrical charge is transferred as follows:

- negative ions (**anions**) move to the anode and lose electrons
- the electrons travel around the circuit to the cathode
- at the cathode, electrons are transferred to the positive ions (**cations**).

> **Key Point**

When drawing the circuit, the battery or power pack must be shown as two vertical lines: the longer line is the positive terminal, the shorter line is the negative terminal.

The products formed during the electrolysis of certain electrolytes are shown:

Electrolyte	Product at the cathode	Product at the anode
Molten lead(II) bromide	Lead (a silvery solid forms)	Bromine (a brown gas forms)
Concentrated aqueous sodium chloride	Hydrogen (a colourless gas forms)	Chlorine (a pungent gas forms)
Dilute sulfuric acid	Hydrogen (a colourless gas forms)	Oxygen (a colourless gas forms)

> **Key Point**
>
> Metals or hydrogen form at the cathode (see Reactivity series on pages 78–79). Non-metals (other than hydrogen) form at the anode.

S In an aqueous solution, as well as the ions from the compound, there will be a small quantity of ions from the water: $H_2O(l) \rightarrow H^+(aq) + OH^-(aq)$.

In a dilute solution, oxygen will usually form at the anode from the discharge of the OH^- ions.

Electrolyte	Product at the cathode	Product at the anode
Aqueous copper(II) sulfate with carbon electrodes	Copper deposited $Cu^{2+}(aq) + 2e^- \rightarrow Cu(s)$	Oxygen gas given off $4OH^-(aq) \rightarrow 2H_2O(l) + O_2(g) + 4e^-$
Aqueous copper(II) sulfate with copper electrodes	Copper deposited $Cu^{2+}(aq) + 2e^- \rightarrow Cu(s)$	The copper dissolves $Cu(s) \rightarrow Cu^{2+}(aq) + 2e^-$
Dilute sodium chloride solution	Hydrogen gas given off $2H^+(aq) + 2e^- \rightarrow H_2(g)$	Oxygen gas given off $4OH^-(aq) \rightarrow 2H_2O(l) + O_2(g) + 4e^-$

A metal can be coated with another metal in a process called **electroplating**. Electroplating can improve the appearance of the metal or provide resistance to corrosion. For example, iron can be coated with silver.

- The metal to be coated is made the cathode (in the example, iron).
- The coating metal is made the anode (in the example, silver).
- The electrolyte contains ions of the coating metal (in the example, aqueous silver nitrate).

Hydrogen–oxygen fuel cells

Hydrogen and oxygen can be used to produce electricity in a fuel cell. The only chemical product is water.

S Compared to producing electricity by burning coal or oil, one advantage of the hydrogen–oxygen **fuel cell** is that no carbon dioxide is produced in the reaction to produce electricity, and so there is no impact on global warming. The disadvantage is that, carbon dioxide is produced, which contributes to global warming.

> **Quick Test**
>
> 1. Explain why an electrolyte must be molten or in aqueous solution.
>
> S 2. A dilute solution of potassium bromide is electrolysed.
>   a) Explain why hydrogen gas is formed at the cathode instead of potassium.
>   b) Write an ionic equation showing the formation of the hydrogen gas.

Exothermic and endothermic reactions

Syllabus links:
5.1.1–5.1.3,
S 5.1.4–5.1.8

Learning aims:

- Define exothermic and endothermic reactions.
- Interpret reaction pathway diagrams.
- **S** Define enthalpy change and activation energy.
- **S** Perform calculations involving bond energies.

Exothermic and endothermic reactions

An **exothermic reaction** transfers thermal energy to the surroundings.
This causes an increase in the temperature of the surroundings.

An **endothermic reaction** takes in thermal energy from the surroundings.
This leads to a decrease in the temperature of the surroundings.

> ## Practical skills

The apparatus below can be used to identify whether a reaction is exothermic or endothermic and to compare different reactions.

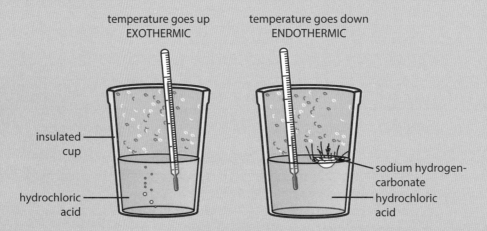

temperature goes up
EXOTHERMIC

temperature goes down
ENDOTHERMIC

insulated cup

hydrochloric acid

sodium hydrogen-carbonate

hydrochloric acid

In reactions which do not involve any heating it is very important to use an insulated cup (for example a polystyrene cup). This will reduce the transfer of thermal energy:

- from the reaction to the surroundings in an exothermic reaction
- from the surroundings to the reaction in an endothermic reaction.

> ## Practical skills

The apparatus below can be used to compare the energy produced by burning different liquid fuels.

The draught excluders are used to make sure as much thermal energy as possible is transferred to the water in the metal can. A metal can is used as it is a good conductor of heat and will transfer most of the energy to the water.

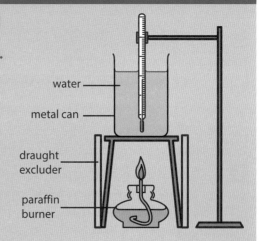

water

metal can

draught excluder

paraffin burner

Reaction pathway diagrams

These can be used to show whether a reaction is exothermic or endothermic.

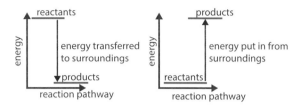

S The transfer of thermal energy during a reaction is called the **enthalpy change**, ΔH, of the reaction. In a reaction pathway diagram, if the energy of the reactants is greater than the energy of the products, then the reaction is exothermic and ΔH is negative. If the energy of the reactants is lower than the energy of the products, the reaction is endothermic and ΔH is positive.

A reaction pathway diagram can also be drawn to show the minimum energy that has to be available for a reaction to take place (see Fig. 5.1). This minimum energy is called the **activation energy**, E_a.

S Bond energies

For a reaction to take place, the bonds in the reactants must be broken and the bonds in the products must be formed. This bond breaking and forming will determine whether the reaction is exothermic or endothermic. **Bond energies**, measured in kJ/mol, can be used to calculate the enthalpy change in a reaction. An example of a bond energy calculation is shown in the table below.

Example 1 Hydrogen reacts with oxygen to form water. Calculate the enthalpy change in the reaction.

Steps in the calculation	Calculation
Write down the equation	$2H_2(g) + O_2(g) \rightarrow 2H_2O(l)$
Use the bond energies for the bonds broken and formed in the reaction	H–H 436 kJ/mol O=O 498 kJ/mol H–O 464 kJ/mol
Calculate the total energy needed to break bonds (+ve as endothermic)	$2H–H = 2 \times 436 = +872$ kJ/mol= $1O=O = 1 \times 498 = +498$ kJ/mol Total $= 872 + 498 = +1370$ kJ/mol
Calculate the total energy released when bonds are made (–ve as exothermic)	$4H–O = 4 \times 464 = -1856$ kJ/mol
Calculate the difference between bond breaking and bond forming	$1370 - 1856 = -486$ kJ/mol $\Delta H = -486$ kJ/mol

> **Quick Test**

1. Define what is meant by an endothermic reaction.
S 2. Define activation energy, E_a.

Physical and chemical changes, rate of reaction

Syllabus links:
6.1.1, 6.2.1–6.2.4 ,
S 6.2.5–6.2.8

Learning aims:

- Identify physical and chemical changes.
- Describe the factors that can change the rate of a reaction.
- Describe practical methods for measuring the rate of reactions.
- **S** Use collision theory to explain how factors can change the rate of a reaction.
- **S** Evaluate practical methods for investigating rates of reaction.

A **physical change** does not change the chemical substance itself. It may involve a change of state, for example when sodium chloride dissolves in water to form a solution.

In a **chemical change** one or more new substances are produced. In most cases an energy change is linked to the chemical change, for example when magnesium burns in oxygen to form magnesium oxide.

Factors affecting rate of reaction

A number of factors can affect the rate of a reaction. These include changing:

- the concentration of solutions
- the pressure of gases
- the surface area of solids
- the temperature
- adding or removing a catalyst or enzyme.

For a reaction to occur the particles in the reactants must collide.

The rate of a reaction changes as the reaction proceeds. In nearly all cases the rate of reaction decreases during the reaction as the reactants get used up.

> **Key Point**
>
> A **catalyst** or **enzyme** increases the rate of a reaction but remains unchanged at the end of the reaction.

> **Key Point**
>
> If a reaction is exothermic, it is possible that the rate of reaction could increase as the reaction occurs. The thermal energy produced causes the temperature to rise, which increases the rate of reaction.

> **Practical skills**
>
> The rate of a reaction can be measured by measuring the change in mass (Fig. 6.1).

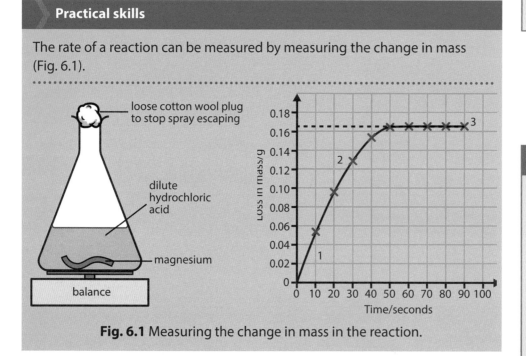

Fig. 6.1 Measuring the change in mass in the reaction.

> **Key Point**
>
> The gradient of the curve is greatest at the start as the maximum number of reacting particles are present. As the particles react, the gradient gets less steep. Eventually the rate of the reaction is zero; the curve levels out, as at least one of the reactants has been used up.

Practical skills

The rate of a reaction can also be measured by measuring the volume of gas as it is produced in a reaction (Fig. 6.2).

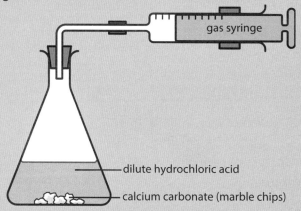
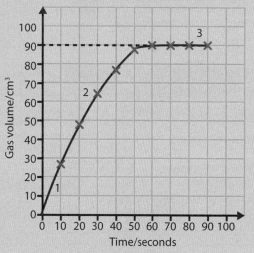

Fig. 6.2 Measuring the rate of reaction between calcium carbonate and hydrochloric acid.

S The changes in the rate of a reaction can be explained using **collision theory**.

Factors affecting rate of reaction	To increase the rate of reaction	Explanation in terms of collision theory
Concentration of a solution	Increase concentration	More particles in a fixed volume of solution – greater frequency of collisions
Pressure of gases	Increase the pressure	Particles closer together – greater frequency of collisions
Surface area of solids	Increase surface area	More reacting particles – greater frequency of collisions
Temperature	Increase temperature	Greater kinetic energy of particles
Catalyst or enzyme	Add a catalyst or enzyme	Lowers the activation energy, E_a

> ## Key Point
>
> Check Exothermic and endothermic reactions on pages 44–45 if you need to revise activation energy.

Quick Test

1. Describe the effect of temperature on the rate of reaction.
2. **a)** Would you expect the rate of a reaction to increase or decrease as the reaction proceeds?
   S b) Explain your answer using collision theory.
3. In a reaction between magnesium and hydrochloric acid:
   a) What effect will increasing the concentration of the acid have on the rate of the reaction?
   S b) Explain your answer.
   c) Look at the apparatus on the previous page used to measure the change in mass in this reaction. Evaluate the main sources of error in this experiment.

Reversible reactions and equilibrium

Syllabus links: 6.3.1–6.3.2, S 6.3.3–6.3.11

Learning aims:

- Describe how changing conditions affect a reversible reaction.
- S State what equilibrium is in a reversible reaction.
- S Explain how particular conditions affect the position of equilibrium in a reversible reaction.
- S State and explain the conditions used in the Haber and Contact industrial processes.

Reversible reactions

Reversible reactions are shown by the symbol $\rightleftharpoons$.

Copper(II) sulfate crystals are **hydrated** and contain **water of crystallisation**. When heated, the hydrated blue crystals lose the water of crystallisation and form an **anhydrous** white powder. The reaction can be reversed by adding water to the white powder:

$$CuSO_4.5H_2O(s) \rightleftharpoons CuSO_4(s) + 5H_2O(l)$$

copper(II) sulfate crystals   copper(II) sulfate powder + water

      blue   white

Hydrated cobalt(II) chloride crystals undergo a similar reversible reaction. Heating the crystals produces anhydrous cobalt(II) chloride and adding water to the anhydrous powder reverses the reaction:

$$CoCl_2.6H_2O(s) \rightleftharpoons CoCl_2(s) + 6H_2O(l)$$

cobalt(II) chloride crystals   cobalt(II) chloride powder + water

      pink   blue

S Equilibrium

If a reversible reaction is in a closed system (one where chemicals cannot escape or enter), an **equilibrium** is established. The rate of the forward reaction is equal to the rate of the reverse reaction. This means that, at equilibrium, the concentrations or amounts of reactants and products are no longer changing.

Reversible reactions might seem to be inconvenient in the chemical industry. The product being made is constantly changing back to the reactants. Fortunately, changes can be made to the position of the equilibrium by changing the conditions under which the reaction occurs.

S Production of ammonia

Ammonia is manufactured in the **Haber process** from nitrogen (from the air) and hydrogen (from methane). The table shows how a balance is reached in the reaction: $N_2(g) + 3H_2(g) \rightleftharpoons 2NH_3(g)$ $\Delta H = -ve$

> **Key Point**
>
> In an equilibrium, the amounts of reactants and products do not have to be the same. It is usually not equally balanced. Think of a see-saw that is not perfectly balanced – it is not horizontal.

> **Key Point**
>
> You may need to check the topic on chemical energetics and enthalpy change, ΔH, on pages 44–45

Changes made to the reversible reaction	Result of the changes
Increasing temperature	As $\Delta H = -ve$ (exothermic), this favours the endothermic/ reverse reaction. Equilibrium moves to N_2 and H_2

Pressure of reacting gases	Equilibrium moves to reactants or products with the fewer molecules.
	Equilibrium moves to NH_3

When making ammonia in industry, a balance needs to be struck between the conditions that favour the formation of the ammonia and how quickly it is made. The rate of reaction is a crucial factor. The table shows how a balance is reached in the reaction: $N_2(g) + 3H_2(g) \rightleftharpoons 2NH_3(g)$ $\Delta H = -ve$

Ideal equilibrium conditions	Ideal rate conditions	Actual conditions used
High pressure	High pressure	20 000 kPa (200 atm)
Low temperature	High temperature	450°C
No need for a catalyst	Use a catalyst	Catalyst = iron

s Production of sulfuric acid

A key part of the manufacture of sulfuric acid in the **Contact process** involves the reaction: $2SO_2(g) + O_2(g) \rightleftharpoons 2SO_3(g)$ $\Delta H = -ve$

Sulfur dioxide is obtained by burning sulfur or by roasting sulfide ores.

Oxygen is obtained from the air.

> **Key Point**
>
> The units for pressure are kilopascal (kPa) and standard atmosphere (atm).

Ideal equilibrium conditions	Ideal rate conditions	Actual conditions used
High pressure	High pressure	200 kPa (2 atm)
Low temperature	High temperature	450°C
No need for a catalyst	Use a catalyst	Catalyst = vanadium(V) oxide

In both the industrial processes shown above, it is essential to take safety and economic considerations into account. Therefore, there are limits set on the pressures and temperatures used. High pressures and temperatures will make the process less safe and will also increase the costs of manufacture.

> **Quick Test**
>
> 1. Describe how the reversible reaction between hydrated copper(II) sulfate and anhydrous copper(II) sulfate can be changed by changing the conditions.
>
> s 2. A reversible reaction involves $X(g) + 3Y(g) \rightleftharpoons W(g)$ $\Delta H = +ve$
>   Explain the effect on the equilibrium in this reaction of the following changes:
>   a) increasing temperature
>   b) reducing pressure
>   c) adding a catalyst.
>
> s 3. In the Haber process state the source of the following:
>   a) nitrogen
>   b) hydrogen.

Redox

Syllabus links:
6.4.1–6.4.5,
S 6.4.6–6.4.13

Learning aims:

- Identify redox reactions as reactions involving simultaneous oxidation and reduction.
- S Define oxidation and reduction in terms of electron and oxidation number loss or gain.
- S Explain oxidation and reduction in terms of oxidation numbers.
- S Identify oxidising and reducing agents.

Redox reactions

Redox reactions involve simultaneous **oxidation** and **reduction**.

Oxidation numbers of elements or elements in compounds are identified using Roman numerals. For example, in copper(II) sulfate, copper has an oxidation number of +2.

Redox reactions involve the loss of oxygen (reduction) and the gain of oxygen (oxidation).

Example 1 An example of a redox reaction is shown in the table:	
$Mg(s) + PbO(s) \rightarrow MgO(s) + Pb(s)$	
$Mg \rightarrow MgO$ magnesium has gained oxygen	oxidation
$PbO \rightarrow Pb$ lead(II) oxide has lost oxygen	reduction

S Important information about oxidation numbers:

Elements in their uncombined state have an oxidation number of zero.

Monatomic ions (for example, Na^+, Cl^-) have an oxidation number the same as the charge on the ion.

The sum of the oxidation numbers in a compound is zero.

The sum of the oxidation numbers in an ion (for example, SO_4^{2-}) is equal to the charge on the ion.

Redox reactions involve:

- an increase in oxidation numbers (oxidation) and a decrease in oxidation numbers (reduction)
- the loss of electrons (oxidation) and the gain of electrons (reduction).

S Oxidising and reducing agents

An **oxidising agent** is a substance that oxidises another substance and is itself reduced.

A **reducing agent** is a substance that reduces another substance and is itself oxidised.

Example 2

$2Fe_2O_3(s) + 3C(s) \rightarrow 4Fe(s) + 3CO_2(g)$	
Fe_2O_3 contains Fe^{3+} ions $\rightarrow$ Fe Oxidation number +3 Oxidation number 0 Gained 3 electrons Fe_2O_3 is an oxidising agent and is reduced to Fe	Decrease in oxidation number Addition of electrons Reduction
C $\rightarrow$ CO_2 Oxidation number 0 Oxidation number +4 Lost 4 electrons C is a reducing agent and is oxidised to CO_2	Increase in oxidation number Loss of electrons Oxidation

Redox reactions often involve colour changes.

- Acidified potassium manganate(VII) is a powerful oxidising agent and is reduced in a reaction with a reducing agent (see Fig. 6.3):

$$MnO_4^-(aq) \qquad \rightarrow \qquad Mn^{2+}(aq)$$

purple solution   colourless solution

oxidation number = +7   oxidation number = +2

reduction

- Potassium iodide solution is a reducing agent and is oxidised in a redox reaction:

$$2I^-(aq) \qquad \rightarrow \qquad I_2(aq) + 2e^-$$

colourless solution   dark orange solution

oxidation number = −1   oxidation number = 0

oxidation

> **Key Point**
>
> You may need to revise ionic equations on page 23.

> **Quick Test**
>
> 1. Define reduction in terms of oxygen gain or loss.
> 2. Use the equation to answer the questions below.
> $$2Al(s) + 3CuO(s) \rightarrow Al_2O_3(s) + 3Cu(s)$$
>   a) Identify the substance that has been oxidised in the reaction.
>   b) Identify the substance that has been reduced in the reaction.
> **S** 3. Define oxidation in terms of electron loss or gain.
> **S** 4. Use the equation below to answer the questions below.
> $$Mg(s) + Cu^{2+}(aq) \rightarrow Mg^{2+}(aq) + Cu(s)$$
>   a) What is the oxidation number of Mg?
>   b) What has been oxidised in the reaction?
>   c) What is the reducing agent?

The characteristic properties of acids and bases

Syllabus links:
7.1.1–7.1.8,
S 7.1.9–7.1.12

Learning aims:

- Describe the properties of acids, bases and alkalis.
- Describe hydrogen ion concentration and the neutralisation reaction.
- **S** Know that acids can be described as proton donors and bases as proton acceptors.
- **S** Define strong and weak acids in terms of hydrogen ion concentration.

Acids and bases

An **acid** contains H^+ ions in aqueous solution.

The common acids are hydrochloric acid (HCl), sulfuric acid (H_2SO_4) and nitric acid (HNO_3).

S Ethanoic acid has the formula CH_3COOH.

A **base** is the oxide or hydroxide of a metal. A soluble base is known as an **alkali**. Aqueous solutions of alkalis contain OH^- ions.

S An acid is a proton donor. A base is a proton acceptor.

Indicators and the pH scale

Acids and bases can be identified using **indicators**, as shown in the table.

Indicator	Acid solution	Alkaline solution
Litmus	Red	Blue
Thymolphthalein	Colourless	Blue
Methyl orange	Red	Yellow
Universal indicator	pH < 7	pH > 7

The concentration of hydrogen ions can be measured using universal indicator paper and the **pH scale**. The colour the indicator shows on testing a solution can be matched to the pH scale of numbers, which is shown in the table.

pH scale	Identification	Hydrogen ion concentration
0–6	Acid	From pH 0 to 6 the strength of the acid decreases
7	Neutral	
8–14	Alkali	From pH 8 to 14 the strength of the alkali increases

Reactions of acids and bases

When an acid reacts with a base or an alkali a **salt** is formed.

The typical reactions of acids are shown in the table.

Reaction with an acid	Formed in the reaction	Example
Metals	A salt and hydrogen	$Mg(s) + 2HCl(aq) \rightarrow MgCl_2(aq) + H_2(g)$
Bases and alkalis	A salt and water	$CuO(s) + H_2SO_4(aq) \rightarrow CuSO_4(aq) + H_2O(l)$ $2NaOH(aq) + H_2SO_4(aq) \rightarrow Na_2SO_4(aq) + H_2O(l)$
Carbonates	A salt, carbon dioxide and water	$CaCO_3(s) + 2HNO_3(aq) \rightarrow Ca(NO_3)_2(aq) + CO_2(g) + H_2O(l)$

As well as the reactions shown above, bases and alkalis react with ammonium compounds to form ammonia gas. The equation below shows an example of this reaction:

$$NH_4Cl(s) + NaOH(aq) \rightarrow NaCl(aq) + NH_3(g) + H_2O(l)$$

When an acid (contains H^+ ions) reacts with an alkali (contains OH^- ions) to produce water, the reaction is called a **neutralisation reaction**. The equation for the reaction between sulfuric acid and sodium hydroxide is shown in the table above. This reaction can also be represented using an ionic equation:

$$H^+(aq) + OH^-(aq) \rightarrow H_2O(l)$$

S The strength of an acid is determined by how much the acid dissociates into ions when in aqueous solution. A **strong acid** is fully dissociated into ions. A **weak acid** is only partially dissociated into ions.

Acid	Type of acid	Equation
Hydrochloric acid	Strong	$HCl(aq) \rightarrow H^+(aq) + Cl^-(aq)$
Ethanoic acid	Weak	$CH_3COOH(aq) \rightleftharpoons CH_3COO^-(aq) + H^+(aq)$

> **Key Point**
>
> You will study the formation of salts on pages 54–55, as well as the practical details for preparing a salt that could be part of the examination practical assessment.

> **Key Point**
>
> You may already be familiar with the tests for identifying hydrogen, carbon dioxide and ammonia. You will study the identification of these and other gases in Identification of ions and gases on pages 122–123, and this could form part of the examination practical assessment.

> **Quick Test**
>
> 1. State what colour is formed if thymolphthalein indicator is added to a solution of sodium hydroxide.
> 2. Hydrochloric acid reacts with zinc oxide.
>   a) What type of chemical is zinc oxide?
>   b) Write an equation with state symbols for this reaction.
>   **S** c) State whether hydrochloric acid is a proton donor or proton acceptor.
> 3. Hydrochloric acid and ethanoic acid are both common acids.
>   **S** a) State in what way these two acids are different.
>   b) 0.1M solutions of both acids are tested with universal indicator. Explain the difference in pH values that are recorded.

Oxides and preparation of salts

Learning aims:

* Classify and identify oxides as acidic or basic.
* **S** Classify and identify amphoteric oxides.
* Describe the preparation, separation and purification of soluble salts.
* Describe the solubility rules for salts.
* Define hydrated and anhydrous substances.
* **S** Describe the preparation of insoluble salts.
* **S** Define the term water of crystallisation.

Syllabus links:

7.2.1, **S** 7.2.2–7.2.3
7.3.1–7.3.3,
S 7.3.4–7.3.5

The oxides of non-metal elements are **acidic oxides**. The oxides of metals are **basic oxides**.

An acidic oxide will react with an alkali to form a salt and water. For example:

$$CO_2(g) + Ca(OH)_2 \rightarrow CaCO_3(s) + H_2O(l)$$

A basic oxide will react with an acid to form a salt and water. For example:

$$ZnO(s) + 2HCl(aq) \rightarrow ZnCl_2(aq) + H_2O(l)$$

> **S** **Amphoteric oxides** will react with acids and alkalis to form salts and water. Examples of amphoteric oxides include aluminium oxide, Al_2O_3, and zinc oxide, ZnO.

> **Key Point**
>
> This reaction is used to test for the presence of carbon dioxide. A solution of calcium hydroxide is often called limewater. The cloudiness that forms in the limewater is caused by the formation of calcium carbonate.

Solubility of salts

Before deciding how to make a salt, you need to know if the salt is soluble or insoluble, as shown in the table.

Salts	Soluble	Insoluble
Sodium, potassium, ammonium	Yes	
Nitrates	Yes	
Chlorides	Most	Lead, silver
Sulfates	Most	Barium, calcium, lead
Carbonates	Sodium, potassium, ammonium	Most
Hydroxides	Sodium, potassium, ammonium Calcium (partially)	Most

Preparation of soluble salts

Soluble salts can be prepared by adding the following types of solids to an aqueous solution of the acid:

- metal
- insoluble base
- insoluble carbonate.

For each type of solid the process is the same, as shown in the table.

Stage	Procedure
1	Add solid to acid until in excess.
2	Filter off the excess solid.
3	Evaporate the solution until it is saturated. Leave to crystallise.

Examples of the reactions are shown below:

Metal: $Mg(s) + H_2SO_4(aq) \rightarrow MgSO_4(s) + H_2(g)$

Insoluble base: $CuO(s) + 2HNO_3(aq) \rightarrow Cu(NO_3)_2(s) + H_2O(l)$

Insoluble carbonate: $ZnCO_3(s) + 2HCl(aq) \rightarrow ZnCl_2(s) + CO_2(g) + H_2O(l)$

> **Key Point**
>
> Remember that an alkali is a soluble base.

Titration (see Section 12, pages 118-121)

Another type of preparation for a soluble salt involves a process known as **titration**. This involves the reaction between an acid and an alkali.

> **Key Point**
>
> You may be asked about titrations for the examination practical assessment.

Preparation of insoluble salts

S An **insoluble salt** can be prepared by **precipitation**, where two solutions react to form a solid. For example, two solutions of soluble salts, or aqueous acids or alkalis.

Stage	Procedure
1	Mix the two solutions.
2	Filter the mixture to separate the precipitate (the insoluble salt).
3	Wash the precipitate with a little water.
4	Leave to dry.

Some salts are **hydrated**, meaning the compound is chemically combined with water. Salts where no water is chemically combined are **anhydrous**.

S The water chemically combined with a salt is called **water of crystallisation**. Examples of hydrated salts include $CuSO_4 5H_2$ and $CoCl_2 6H_2O$.

> **Quick Test**
>
> 1. State whether sodium oxide, Na_2O, is acidic or basic.
> **S** 2. Explain the difference between a basic oxide and an amphoteric oxide.
> 3. When making a soluble salt, what must be done to the solution of the salt before it will crystallise?
> **S** 4. When making an insoluble salt, what name is given to the solid that forms when two solutions are mixed?
> **S** 5. What name is given to the water that is chemically combined to a salt?

Electrolysis and hydrogen–oxygen fuel cells

1   Consider the diagram of a circuit used in electrolysis.

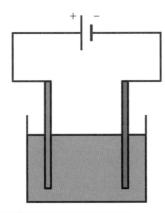

'Consider' means review and respond to given information.

a   Label the anode.   [1]

b   Label the cathode.   [1]

[Total marks 2]

2   **a**   Complete the following table to show the products of electrolysis.

Electrolyte	Product at the anode	Product at the cathode	
Molten lead(II) bromide			[2]
Dilute sulfuric acid			[2]

b   State what material can be used as the electrodes in the above examples of electrolysis.   [1]

[Total marks 5]

3   The inner lining of food containers is often made from steel electroplated with tin. Explain why electroplating is used.   [1]

4   State which of the following is the **only** chemical product of a hydrogen–oxygen fuel cell.

   A.   Carbon dioxide

   B.   Hydrogen

   C.   Oxygen

   D.   Water   [1]

S   **5**   In the electrolysis of molten aluminium oxide:

   a   State the product at the cathode.   [1]

   b   Write an ionic half-equation showing the formation of this product.   [2]

[Total marks 3]

6 **a** Complete the following table.

Electrolyte	Product at the anode	Product at the cathode	
Dilute aqueous sodium iodide			[2]
Concentrated aqueous sodium iodide			[2]

b Write an ionic half-equation for the formation of the product at the anode during the electrolysis of concentrated aqueous sodium iodide. [2]

[Total marks 6]

7 State what you would observe in the electrolysis of copper(II) sulfate using copper electrodes.

a At the anode: **b** At the cathode: [1]

[Total marks 2]

Exothermic and endothermic reactions

1 **a** Define the term exothermic reaction. [2]

'Define' means give the precise meaning.

b Magnesium ribbon reacts with dilute hydrochloric acid at room temperature to form magnesium chloride and hydrogen. The reaction is exothermic.

   i) Write a balanced equation for this reaction. [2]

   ii) What container should be used in a reaction like this? Justify your answer. [2]

'Justify' means support your choice with evidence.

   iii) Three groups of students performed this experiment. Each group used 50 cm^3 of dilute hydrochloric acid but with different masses of magnesium. The results of the three experiments are shown below.

      Complete the last column in the table.

Group	Mass of magnesium (g)	Temperature change (°C)	Temperature change per gram of magnesium (°C/g)	
A	0.5	+15		[1]
B	0.4	+10		[1]
C	0.6	+18		[1]

   iv) One group used the wrong container for the reaction. Suggest which group. [1]

[Total marks 10]

S 2 In photosynthesis carbon dioxide and water react to form glucose and oxygen. The reaction is endothermic.

a Sketch and label a reaction pathway diagram. [2]

b Define the term activation energy, E_a. [1]

[Total marks 3]

S 3 Propane burns in oxygen to form carbon dioxide and water.

Deduce the balanced symbol equation and hence work out the enthalpy change, ΔH, for the reaction. [6]

> **Show me**

Write the equation	$O\ mm2\ CH_3OH + 3O_2 \rightarrow 2CO_2 + 4H_2O$
Work out the energy need to break the bonds. $\Delta H = +ve$	$8\ C-H =$ .... $2\ C-C =$ .... $5\ O = O =$ .... $total = +$ ....
Work out the energy released on forming the bonds.	$6\ C = O =$ .... $8\ O-H =$ .... $total = +$ ....
Add the two energy changes together to get	$+$ .... $-$ ....
DΔH for the reaction.	$DH =$ .... kJ/mol

Do not forget the $+$ and $-$ signs.

Physical and chemical changes, rates of reaction

1 State which of the following describes a physical change.

    A. Adding magnesium to hydrochloric acid.

    B. Burning methane in a Bunsen burner.

    C. Carbon combining with oxygen to form carbon dioxide.

    D. Dissolving copper(II) sulfate in water. [1]

2 State which of the following will not increase the rate of the reaction between marble chips (calcium carbonate) and hydrochloric acid.

    A. Increasing the concentration of the hydrochloric acid.

    B. Increasing the temperature of the hydrochloric acid.

    C. Performing the reaction in a fume cupboard.

    D. Using smaller marble chips. [1]

3 You have to measure the change in mass during the reaction between marble chips and dilute hydrochloric acid. The equation for the reaction is:

$$CaCO_3(s) + 2HCl(aq) \rightarrow CaCl_2(aq) + CO_2(g) + H_2O(l)$$

You use 5 g of marble chips to 50 cm^3 of dilute hydrochloric acid.

a Sketch and label the apparatus you could use. [2]

b You have been told to measure the mass of the reaction vessel every 10 seconds for 1 minute and work out the loss in mass for each reading. Sketch the table you would use to record your results. [2]

c Sketch and label the shape of the graph you would expect if you plotted loss in mass (g) against time (s). [2]

[Total marks 6]

4 Use kinetic particle theory to explain the following changes to the rate of reaction between magnesium ribbon and dilute sulfuric acid:

a Increasing temperature. [2]

b Increasing the concentration of the sulfuric acid. [2]

c Using magnesium powder instead of magnesium ribbon. [2]

[Total marks 6]

'Explain' means make the relationships between things clear.

S 5 Magnesium reacts with dilute sulfuric acid to produce hydrogen. Experiments are carried out with acid temperatures of 30°C and 50°C. The results have been plotted on the graph below:

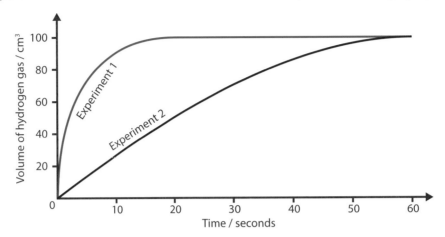

a In one experiment, the temperature of the acid was 50°C. Deduce which experiment. [1]

'Deduce' means make a conclusion from available information.

b Explain why you chose this experiment. [2]

c Explain using collision theory why part of the line for Experiment 1 is horizontal. [2]

[**Total marks 5**]

S 6 Look at the reaction pathway diagram shown.

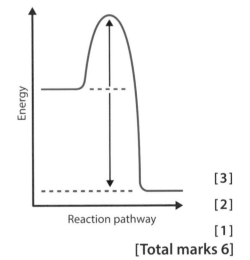

a Add the following labels to the diagram:

  i) reactants _____

  ii) products

  iii) enthalpy change, ΔH

  iv) activation energy, E_a. [3]

b Explain activation energy using collision theory. [2]

c State the effect a catalyst has on the activation energy. [1]

[**Total marks 6**]

Reversible reactions and equilibrium

1 Cobalt(II) chloride crystals have the formula $CoCl_2.6H_2O$. On heating cobalt(II) chloride, powder is formed. This process can be reversed by adding water. State which of the following statements is true. [1]

  A. Cobalt(II) chloride crystals are anhydrous.

  B. Cobalt(II) chloride crystals are blue.

  C. Cobalt(II) chloride crystals contain water of crystallisation.

  D. Cobalt(II) chloride powder is pink.

2 If a reversible reaction is in a closed system, then an equilibrium is established. Explain the effect of the equilibrium on:

a The rates of the forward and reverse reactions. [1]

b The concentrations of reactants and products. [1]

[Total marks 2]

3 Ammonia is manufactured in industry from nitrogen gas and hydrogen gas. The reaction is reversible.

a Write a fully balanced equation for this reaction. [2]

b State the sources of nitrogen and hydrogen.

   i) Nitrogen [1]

   ii) Hydrogen [1]

c The enthalpy change for the formation of ammonia, ΔH, is negative. Complete the table below Indicating the conditions needed to move the equilibrium towards the ammonia. Put ticks in the table to show your choice.

Conditions	High	Low
Temperature			[1]
Pressure			[1]

d A catalyst is used in this reaction.

   i) Name the catalyst [1]

   ii) Explain the effect this catalyst will have on the position of the equilibrium. [1]

[Total marks 8]

4 Sulfur trioxide is manufactured in the Contact process by the reaction of sulfur dioxide with oxygen. The reaction is reversible.

a Write a fully balanced equation for the reaction. [2]

b State the conditions used in this process.

   i) Temperature [1]

   ii) Pressure [1]

   iii) Catalyst [1]

[Total marks 5]

5 Explain why in some equilibrium reactions a high temperature is used even though the equilibrium position is favoured by a low temperature. [2]

Redox

1 ▸ In the compounds shown, which metal does **not** have an oxidation number of +2?

   A. Calcium chloride

   B. Copper(II) sulfate

   C. Sodium chloride

   D. Magnesium sulfate [1]

2 ▸ Define a redox reaction. [1]

3 ▸ Examine the following equation:

$$Mg(s) + CuO(s) \rightarrow MgO(s) + Cu(s)$$

a State the formula of the chemical that has been oxidised. [1]

b State the formula of the chemical that has been reduced. [1]

[Total marks 2]

> 'Examine' means investigate closely in detail.

S **4** ▸ Examine the following equation:

$$Ca(s) + Cl_2(g) \rightarrow CaCl_2(s)$$

a State the formula of the chemical that has been oxidised. [1]

b State the change in oxidation number of the chemical identified in part a. [1]

c State the formula of the chemical that has been reduced. [1]

d State the change in oxidation number of the chemical identified in part c. [1]

[Total marks 4]

S **5** ▸ Examine the following ionic equation:

$$Mg(s) + 2Ag^+(aq) \rightarrow Mg^{2+}(aq) + 2Ag(s)$$

a State the formula of the oxidising agent in this reaction. [1]

b State the formula of the reducing agent in this reaction. [1]

[Total marks 2]

S **6** ▸ Examine the following equation:

$$MnO_4^-(aq) + 8H^+(aq) \rightarrow Mn^{2+}(aq) + 4H_2O(l)$$

a What is the colour change in this reaction? [1]

b What is the change in the oxidation number of the manganese in the reaction? [1]

c Has the manganese been oxidised or reduced? [1]

[Total marks 3]

The characteristic properties of acids and bases

1 Methyl orange indicator is added to a solution of nitric acid. Select the colour of the indicator in the nitric acid.

    A. Blue

    B. Colourless

    C. Red

    D. Yellow   **[1]**

2 Universal indicator paper is added to a very dilute solution of sodium hydroxide. Predict the likely pH number of the solution.

    A. 2

    B. 7

    C. 8

    D. 14   **[1]**

> 'Predict' means make a suggestion based on the information given.

3 Hydrochloric acid reacts with potassium hydroxide to form a salt and water.

a State the name of the salt formed.   **[1]**

b State the name of this type of reaction.   **[1]**

c Write an equation for this reaction.   **[2]**

d Write an ionic equation showing the reaction between any acid and any alkali to produce water.   **[2]**

                                                                          [Total marks 6]

4 Select which of these statements about copper(**II**) oxide is true.

    A. It is an alkali.

    B. It is a base.

    C. It is a proton donor.

    D. It is a salt.   **[1]**

3 This question is about hydrochloric acid and ethanoic acid.

a Are acids proton donors or proton acceptors?   **[1]**

b State which of the two acids is a strong acid.   **[1]**

c Define what is meant by the term 'strong acid'.   **[1]**

d Write an ionic equation showing the ions that the hydrochloric acid forms.   **[2]**

                                                                           [Total marks 5]

Oxides and preparation of salts

1 State which of the following is **not** an acidic oxide.

    A. Carbon dioxide

    B. Phosphorus oxide

    C. Sodium oxide

    D. Sulphur dioxide   **[1]**

S 2 State which of the following oxides is an amphoteric oxide.

    A. Aluminium oxide

    B. Calcium oxide

    C. Magnesium oxide

    D. Potassium oxide   **[1]**

3 Which of the following salts is insoluble in water?

    A. Ammonium chloride

    B. Sodium carbonate

    C. Copper(II) nitrate

    D. Silver chloride   **[1]**

4 Some salts are hydrated.

a Define the term hydrated.   **[1]**

b State the term used to define salts that are not hydrated.   **[1]**

                                                        [Total marks 2]

5 Magnesium sulfate crystals can be made by reacting magnesium with dilute sulfuric acid.

a Write an equation, including state symbols, for this reaction.   **[2]**

b Describe the practical details showing how crystals of magnesium sulfate can be made in this reaction.   **[6]**

> **Show me**

It is important to describe each of the three stages of the practical in detail.

Preparation	
Separation	
Purification	

                                                        [Total marks 8]

6 Magnesium sulfate can also be prepared by reacting magnesium carbonate with dilute sulfuric acid.

a State the name of the gas produced in this reaction. [1]

b Write an equation, including state symbols, for this reaction. [2]

[Total marks 3]

7 Sodium chloride can be prepared by reacting an acid with an alkali using a titration procedure.

a State which acid is used. [1]

b State the name of the apparatus used to measure the volume of acid used. [1]

c State which alkali is used. [1]

d State the name of the apparatus used to measure the volume of alkali used. [1]

e An indicator is used so that the exact amounts of acid and alkali can be used when preparing the sodium chloride. State the name of an indicator that could be used and the colour change that occurs. [3]

Name of indicator	Colour in alkali	Colour in acid

[Total marks 7]

8 Lead(II) chloride is an insoluble salt that can be prepared using a precipitation method with dilute hydrochloric acid and lead(II) nitrate solution.

a Define the term precipitate. [1]

b Write a chemical equation, with state symbols, for this reaction. [2]

c Describe how a sample of lead(II) chloride can be prepared in a laboratory. [4]

> **Show me**

It is important to describe each of the three stages of the practical.

Preparation	
Separation	
Purification	

[Total marks 7]

9 Cobalt(II) chloride crystals have the formula $CoCl_2 \cdot 6H_2O$.

a What name is given to the water shown in the formula? [1]

b Explain why the cobalt(II) chloride crystals are a compound and not a mixture. [1]

[Total marks 2]

Arrangement of elements

Syllabus links:

8.1.1–8.1.5, S 8.1.6

Learning aims:

- Describe the Periodic Table in terms of groups and periods, and proton number / atomic number.

- Describe the change from metallic to non-metallic elements across a period and the charge on the ions formed by the elements.

- Explain and predict the chemical properties of the elements in terms of their positions in the Periodic Table.

- S Identify trends in groups.

The elements

The Periodic Table arranges elements in order of increasing **proton number /atomic number**. The elements are arranged in rows (**periods**) and columns (**groups**).

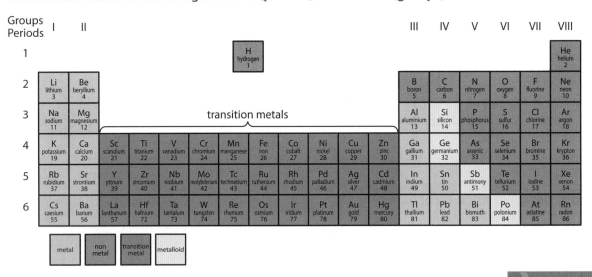

As a general rule, the elements on the left-hand side of the Periodic Table are metals and the elements on the right-hand side of the Periodic Table are non-metals. The main features of the elements as you look across Period 3 are summarised in the table.

> ### Key Point
>
> You will be pleased to know that you do not need to remember the elements in the Periodic Table. In the examinations, a Periodic Table is always provided. You will need to be familiar with some of the elements in certain groups. These are covered in later parts of this section.

> ### Key Point
>
> This section builds on the work studied in Section 2. A quick revision of Atomic structure and the Periodic Table (pages 10–11) could prove very helpful.

Period	Groups							
3	**I**	**II**	**III**	**IV**	**V**	**VI**	**VII**	**VIII**
Element name	Sodium	Magnesium	Aluminium	Silicon	Phosphorus	Sulfur	Chlorine	Argon
Metallic (M) or non-metallic (NM)	M	M	M	NM	NM	NM	NM	NM
Electron configuration of the atom	2,8,1	2,8,2	2,8,3	2,8,4	2,8,5	2,8,6	2,8,7	2,8,8
Charge on the ion	1+	2+	3+	No ions	3−	2−	1−	No ions

Trends in physical and chemical properties of the elements

Elements in the same group of the Periodic Table usually have similar physical and chemical properties. Physical properties include melting and boiling points.

The chemical properties of an element depend on the element's electron arrangement. For example, in a chemical reaction some elements change their electron configuration. So, for example, using the elements in Period 3:

- elements with one, two or three electrons in their outer electron shell lose these electrons and form positive ions
- the element with four electrons in its outer electron shell does not lose or gain electrons
- elements with five, six or seven electrons in their outer electron shell gain electrons and form negative ions
- the element with a full outer electron shell does not usually form compounds.

> **Key Point**

Working out the charges on the ions is covered in more detail in the topic Ions and ionic bonds on pages 14–15. You may need to revise this topic.

S Within a group there will be trends or changes in the properties of the elements. For example, the diagrams show some of the trends in Group VII.

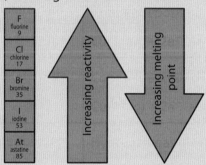

> **Quick Test**

1. Define what is meant by a period of the Periodic Table.
2. State which is more likely to be a non-metal, an element in Group II or an element in Group V.
3. An element has a proton number of 16.
   a) Deduce the electron configuration of this element.
   b) Deduce the charge on the ion formed by this element.
S 4. Examine the table, which contains data for the Group VIII elements. Identify the trend in these boiling points (temperatures are in degrees Celsius, °C).

Element	Boiling point (°C)
He	−269
Ne	−246
Ar	−186
Kr	−152
Xe	−108
Rn	−62

Group I properties

Learning aims:

- Describe lithium, sodium and potassium as soft metals with properties that show trends down the group.
- Describe trends in properties including melting point, density and reactivity.
- Predict properties of other elements in the group.

Syllabus links: 8.2.1–8.2.2

Physical properties

This is a group of metals but they have properties very different to those of the metals in everyday use in homes and factories. For example, sodium is soft to cut.

The first three members of Group I are shown in the table together with some of their **physical properties**.

Element	Melting point (°C)	Boiling point (°C)	Density (g/cm^3)
Lithium	180	1342	0.53
Sodium	98	883	0.97
Potassium	64	759	0.86

The melting and boiling points decrease as you go down the group.

Generally, the density increases down the group but this is not a consistent trend. For example, sodium is out of step with potassium.

Chemical properties

The Group I elements are highly reactive. For this reason, rubidium and caesium are not available in schools. The electronic configurations of the three elements are shown in the table.

Group I element	Electronic configuration	Ion
Lithium	2,1	Li$^+$
Sodium	2,8,1	Na$^+$
Potassium	2,8,8,1	K$^+$

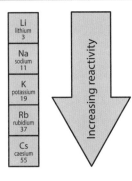

Increasing reactivity

The metals will readily lose one electron in a reaction with a non-metal and form an ion with a single positive charge.

Lithium, sodium and potassium react rapidly with air and water. For this reason, they are stored under oil to prevent contact with air and moisture.

Potassium catches fire when added to water.

> **Key Point**
>
> In the examination it is likely that you will be given data and then asked to predict the properties of rubidium (Rb) and caesium (Cs).

> **Key Point**
>
> You should be familiar with the relationship between group number and the charge on the ion the element forms.

Reaction	Observations	Examples
Air or oxygen	The metals burn easily and the oxides formed produce these colours: lithium – red sodium – orange/yellow potassium – lilac	potassium + oxygen → potassium oxide $4K(s) + O_2(g) \rightarrow 2K_2O(s)$
Water	The metals react rapidly, float on the surface of the water and move around rapidly. With potassium, the hydrogen that is produced catches fire.	sodium + water → sodium hydroxide + hydrogen $2Na(s) + 2H_2O(l) \rightarrow 2NaOH(aq) + H_2(g)$

Key Point

In Section 12 you will learn about how to perform flame tests on metal compounds, on page 123. The colours identify the metals present. You will need to remember the colours produced by lithium, sodium and potassium.

Key Point

In Section 7 you studied alkalis. The sodium hydroxide produced when sodium is added to water is an alkali. For this reason, the Group I elements are sometimes called alkali metals.

Potassium burns in air with a lilac flame.

Quick Test

1. Predict how the melting point of caesium will compare with that of potassium.
2. Predict how the reactivity of rubidium will compare to that of sodium.
3. Write a fully balanced equation, including state symbols, for the reaction between lithium and oxygen.
4. Write a fully balanced equation, including state symbols, for the reaction between potassium and water.

Group VII properties

Syllabus links: 8.3.1–8.3.4

Learning aims:

- Describe chlorine, bromine and iodine as diatomic non-metals with properties that show trends down the group, including their appearance, increasing density and decreasing reactivity.

- Describe and explain displacement reactions.

- Predict the properties of other elements in the group.

Physical properties

Chlorine

Bromine

Iodine

Element	Formula	Appearance	Density
Chlorine	Cl_2	Pale yellow-green gas	↓ Increasing
Bromine	Br_2	Red-brown liquid	
Iodine	I_2	Grey-black solid	

The elements exist as **diatomic** molecules as shown in the table. The states of matter change down the group from gas to liquid to solid. The density of the elements increases down the group. Given this information, it is possible to predict the properties of the other members of the group, including fluorine (F) and astatine (At). For example, fluorine is a gas and astatine is a solid (at room temperature).

Chemical properties

This group includes the most reactive non-metals in the Periodic Table. The elements have seven electrons in their outer electron shell. They achieve a full outer electron shell by forming ionic or covalent bonds. In ionic bonding they form single negative ions, for example Cl^-; in covalent bonding they form single covalent bonds, for example Cl-Cl.

> **Key Point**
>
> These different types of bonding are covered in Section 2 and you may find a quick revision helpful.

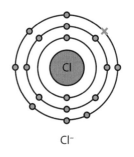
Cl⁻

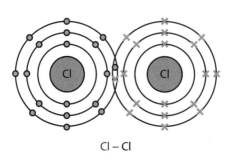
Cl – Cl

The reactivity of the elements is at its greatest at the top of the group.

The elements take part in **displacement reactions**. A more reactive element will displace a less reactive element from a solution of its salt.

Examples of this type of reaction are shown in the table.

Observations	Equations
Chlorine gas will displace bromine when it is bubbled through a solution of the salt, sodium bromide. The colourless sodium bromide solution will turn brown due to the formation of bromine.	chlorine + sodium bromide → sodium chloride + bromine $Cl_2(g) + 2NaBr(aq) \rightarrow 2NaCl(aq) + Br_2(aq)$
Bromine liquid (or aqueous bromine) will displace iodine when added to a solution of sodium iodide. The colourless sodium iodide solution will turn brown due to the formation of iodine.	bromine + sodium iodide → sodium bromide + iodine $Br_2(aq) + 2NaI(aq) \rightarrow 2NaBr(aq) + I_2(aq)$

S The displacement reactions can also be shown using ionic equations:

$Cl_2(g) + 2Br^-(aq) \rightarrow 2Cl^-(aq) + Br_2(aq)$

$Br_2(aq) + 2I^-(aq) \rightarrow 2Br^-(aq) + I_2(aq)$

Fluorine and astatine will also show displacement reactions. Fluorine will displace all other Group VII elements from solutions of their salts. In contrast, astatine will not displace the top four elements in the group from solutions of their salts.

Quick Test

1. Describe the appearance of iodine.
2. State how the density of bromine will compare to that of chlorine.
3. State which is the most reactive element in Group VII.
4. Write an equation, including state symbols, for the displacement reaction between chlorine and sodium iodide solution.

Transition elements and noble gases

Syllabus links:

8.4.1, S 8.4.2 , 8.5.1

Learning aims:

- Describe the characteristics of transition elements and their properties.
- S Describe the variable oxidation states of the transition elements.
- Describe the location of noble gases in the Periodic Table.
- Explain why the noble gases are unreactive, monatomic gases.

Transition elements

The transition elements are grouped in the middle of the Periodic Table between Groups II and III. They are called transition metals because of their position in the Periodic Table and how they are placed between metals on the left and non-metals on the right. Those in the 4th period include many of the well-known metals.

> **Key Point**
>
> Section 9: Metals will provide a more detailed study of metals like these transition elements.

Scandium	Titanium	Vanadium	Chromium	Manganese	Iron	Cobalt	Nickel	Copper	Zinc
Sc	Ti	V	Cr	Mn	Fe	Co	Ni	Cu	Zn

These metals have properties very different to those in Group I. The properties include:

- high densities
- high melting points
- they form coloured compounds
- the elements and their compounds act as catalysts in industrial processes.

In the **Haber process** for the manufacture of ammonia, iron is used as the catalyst. In the Contact process for manufacturing sulfur trioxide vanadium(V) oxide is used as a catalyst.

> **Key Point**
>
> The first three of these properties are very different to those you studied for Group I. It is worth looking back at the Group I properties to see the differences.

S Many of the transition elements have variable **oxidation numbers**. As metals they lose electrons and form positively charged ions. Where the number of electrons they lose in reacting with non-metals can vary, the oxidation number is included in the name of the compounds formed.

> **Key Point**
>
> The Haber and Contact process are part of the topic on Reversible reactions and equilibrium, on pages 48–49. If you have studied this topic you may need to revise the conditions for these industrial processes.

Name of element	Oxidation numbers	Name of compounds	Metal ion formed	Chemical formula of compound
Iron	2	Iron(II) oxide	Fe^{2+}	FeO
	3	Iron(III) oxide	Fe^{3+}	Fe_2O_3
Copper	1	Copper(I) oxide	Cu^+	Cu_2O
	2	Copper(II) oxide	Cu^{2+}	CuO

Noble gases

The noble gases are non-metals. They are unreactive as they have full outer electron shells. With full outer electron shells:

- they do not gain or lose electrons, so do not form ionic bonds
- they do not share electrons, so do not form covalent bonds.

As a result, they are very different from most other non-metals in the Periodic Table.

Element	Symbol	Electronic configuration
Helium	He	2
Neon	Ne	2,8
Argon	Ar	2,8,8

The noble gases are **monatomic** (they exist as single atoms) because they have a complete outer shell of electrons and do not need to form molecules.

> ## Quick Test
>
> 1. How will the melting point of copper compare with sodium?
> 2. Iron acts as a catalyst in the Haber process. Define the term catalyst.
> **S** 3. A laboratory chemical has the formula $KMnO_4$. Calculate the oxidation number of the manganese in this chemical.
> 4. Explain why the noble gases are unreactive.
> 5. Noble gases are monatomic. Explain what this means.

Properties of metals

Syllabus links:
9.1.1–9.1.2

Learning aims:

- Compare the general properties of metals and non-metals.

- Describe the general properties of metals including their reactions with oxygen, dilute acids, cold water and steam.

General physical properties

The general physical properties of metals are summarised in the table and compared with non-metals.

Physical property	Metals (generally)		Non-metals (generally)
Thermal conductivity	Good conductors of heat		Poor conductors of heat
Electrical conductivity	Good conductors of electricity		Poor conductors of electricity
Malleability	Malleable – can be hammered into shape		Brittle when hammered
Ductility	Ductile – can be drawn into wire		Brittle when stretched
Melting and boiling points	Generally high		Generally low

The properties listed above are general properties. This means most, but not all, metals and non-metals have these properties. For example, Group I metals have low melting and boiling points. Similarly, the non-metal carbon (as diamond or graphite) has very high melting and boiling points.

> **Key Point**

You need to be familiar with the terms **thermal conductivity**, **electrical conductivity**, malleable/ **malleability** and **ductile/ductility**.

General chemical properties

Examples of these general chemical properties are shown in the table.

General property	Observations	Equations
Reaction with dilute acids	Effervesence as hydrogen gas produced. The metal dissolves.	magnesium + dilute hydrochloric acid → magnesium chloride + hydrogen $Mg(s) + 2HCl(aq) \rightarrow MgCl_2(aq) + H_2(g)$
Reaction with cold water	Effervescence as hydrogen gas produced. The metal dissolves.	sodium + water → sodium hydroxide + hydrogen $2Na(s) + 2H_2O(l) \rightarrow 2NaOH(aq) + H_2(g)$
Reaction with steam	Hydrogen gas produced. The metal forms a solid oxide.	iron + steam → iron(III) oxide + hydrogen $2Fe(s) + 3H_2O(g) \rightarrow Fe_2O_3(s) + 3H_2(g)$
Reaction with oxygen	On heating the metal forms a solid oxide.	calcium + oxygen → calcium oxide $2Ca(s) + O_2(g) \rightarrow 2CaO(s)$

> ## Key Point
>
> As with the general physical properties, not all metals show these chemical properties. Later in this section you will revise the **reactivity series**, which will provide more detailed information comparing the chemical properties of different metals.

> ## Key Point
>
> Group I metals are highly reactive; they are stored under oil to prevent reaction with water or oxygen. They react with oxygen without needing to be heated and the reaction with steam can be very fast and dangerous.

> ## Quick Test
>
> 1. Copper is often used as the metal in electrical cables. Give **two** physical properties of copper which make it suitable for this use.
> 2. Potassium reacts rapidly with cold water.
>   a) Write a word equation for this reaction.
>   b) Write a chemical equation, with state symbols, for this reaction.
> 3. Zinc reacts with dilute hydrochloric acid. Write a chemical equation, including state symbols, for this reaction.

Uses of metals, alloys and their properties

Syllabus links:
9.2.1, 9.3.1–9.3.4
S 9.3.5

Learning aims:

- Describe the uses of metals in terms of their physical properties.
- Describe and explain the uses of aluminium and copper.
- Describe an alloy as a mixture of a metal with other elements.
- Describe the uses of alloys, including stainless steel and brass, in terms of their physical properties.
- Identify alloys from structural diagrams.
- **S** Explain why alloys can be harder and stronger than pure metals.

Uses of metals

The physical properties of individual metals are the key factor in deciding what they can be used for. The table shows the properties and uses of aluminium and copper.

Metal	Physical property	Use
Aluminium	Low density / Resistance to corrosion	Manufacture of aircraft
	Low density / Good electrical conductivity	Overhead electrical cables
	Resistance to corrosion	Food containers
Copper	Good electrical conductivity / Ductility	Electrical wiring

Alloys and their properties

An **alloy** is a mixture of a metal with one or more other elements.

Some common alloys are mixtures of two metals but some are mixtures of a metal with a non-metal. Alloys can be harder and stronger than pure metals and so can be more useful.

The composition of some common alloys are shown in the table.

Alloy	Composition	Use
Brass	Copper (70%) and zinc (30%)	Locks, hinges, ornaments (corrosion resistance)
Stainless steel	Iron and elements such as chromium, nickel and carbon	Cutlery, kitchen utensils (hardness, resistance to rusting)

> **Key Point**
>
> **Corrosion** is largely due to oxidation by the air in the presence of water.

> **Key Point**
>
> Later in this section you will be able to check the reason why aluminium has a great resistance to corrosion. It forms an oxide layer that prevents air and water from reaching the metal surface.

> **Key Point**
>
> It is important to use the word mixture when defining an alloy. It is **not** a compound – the elements are not chemically bonded together.

The structure of a pure metal is shown in the diagram below alongside that of an alloy.

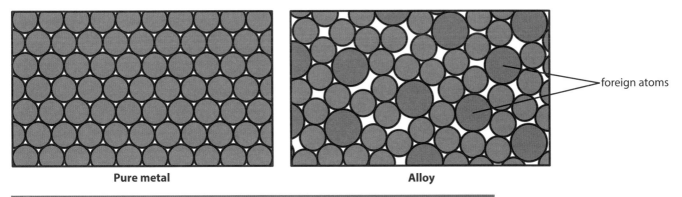

Pure metal   **Alloy**   foreign atoms

> **Key Point**

In an examination you can sketch diagrams like these when answering a question on the structure and strength of alloys. You do not need a compass – the circles of the metal do not need to be exactly the same size in your sketch.

S In a pure metal, atoms are arranged in rows but the rows can slide over each other (they are ductile), or they can separate and the structure can break up (the metal can be brittle).

In contrast, in an alloy the added element breaks up the regular structure and the layers cannot slide over each other. This makes the structure harder and stronger.

> **Quick Test**

1. Explain why iron would not be a good metal for aircraft construction.
2. Define the term ductility.
3. Define the term alloy.
4. State the elements present in brass.

S 5. Use the structure of an alloy to explain why it is stronger than the pure metal.

Reactivity series

Learning aims:

Syllabus links:
9.4.1–9.4.3,
S 9.4.4–9.4.5

- State the order of the reactivity series.
- Describe reactions with cold water, steam and dilute hydrochloric acid.
- Deduce an order of reactivity from experimental results.
- **S** Describe the relative reactivities of the metals in the reactivity series.
- **S** Explain the unreactivity of aluminium.

Order of reactivity of metals

The **reactivity series** shows the order of reactivity of metals.

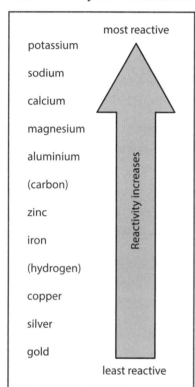

| most reactive |
| potassium |
| sodium |
| calcium |
| magnesium |
| aluminium |
| (carbon) |
| zinc |
| iron |
| (hydrogen) |
| copper |
| silver |
| gold |
| least reactive |

Reactivity increases

Carbon and hydrogen are shown in brackets as these are non-metals.

Carbon will reduce metal oxides of the metals below it but not the metals above it.

Hydrogen is formed when the metals above it react with an acid, such as dilute hydrochloric acid. Metals below hydrogen do not react with dilute acids.

> **Key Point**
>
> The metals that react with cold water will also react with steam and dilute hydrochloric acid, but these reactions are very violent and dangerous.

The reactions of the metals are summarised in the table.

Reaction	Examples of metals in the reactivity series that react	Examples
Cold water	K, Na, Ca	potassium + water → potassium hydroxide + hydrogen $2K(s) + 2H_2O(l) \rightarrow 2KOH(aq) + H_2(g)$
Steam	Mg	magnesium + steam → magnesium oxide + hydrogen $Mg(s) + H_2O(g) \rightarrow MgO(s) + H_2(g)$
Dilute hydrochloric acid	Mg, Zn, Fe	zinc + hydrochloric acid → zinc chloride + hydrogen $Zn(s) + 2HCl(aq) \rightarrow ZnCl_2(aq) + H_2(g)$

S Formation of ions and displacement reactions

When metals react, they lose electrons and form positive ions. The order of metals in the reactivity series shows how readily the metals form these positive ions. The easier it is for a metal to form a positive ion, the more reactive it is.

Metals also take part in **displacement reactions**. In a displacement reaction, a more reactive metal displaces (takes the place of) a less reactive metal from a solution of a salt of the less reactive metal.

Examples of displacement reactions involving metals are shown in the table.

Displacement reaction	Reactivity of the metals
magnesium + zinc chloride solution	$Mg(s) + ZnCl_2(aq) \rightarrow MgCl_2(aq) + Zn(s)$ Magnesium is more reactive than zinc.
zinc + copper(II) sulfate solution	$Zn(s) + CuSO_4(aq) \rightarrow ZnSO_4(aq) + Cu(s)$ Zinc is more reactive than copper.
magnesium + silver nitrate solution	$Mg(s) + 2AgNO_3(aq) \rightarrow Mg(NO_3)_2(aq) + 2Ag(s)$ Magnesium is more reactive than silver.

The position of aluminium in the reactivity series can be difficult to understand. It is in the top third of the reactivity series so it is a reactive metal. However, it is used extensively in situations where a metal is needed but it must resist corrosion. An example would be the use of aluminium in overhead electrical cables.

Aluminium has a thin coating of aluminium oxide all over its surface. This coating prevents corrosion by preventing contact between the aluminium metal and air and water.

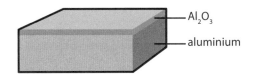

Al_2O_3
aluminium

> ### Key Point
>
> You may have encountered displacement reactions in Group VII properties on page 71. These displacement reactions show the different reactivities of chlorine, bromine and iodine. It might be helpful to revise this.

> ### Key Point
>
> You may want to look back on your revision on the uses of metals on pages 76–77.

> ### Quick Test
>
> 1. Name the most reactive metal in the reactivity series.
> 2. a) Will zinc displace calcium from a solution of calcium chloride?
>   b) Explain your answer.
> S 3. Aluminium is a more reactive metal than iron but iron corrodes in the atmosphere and aluminium does not. Explain why this is.
> S 4. Zinc will displace silver from a solution of silver nitrate. Write a chemical equation, with state symbols, for this reaction.

Corrosion of metals and extraction of metals

Syllabus links:
9.6.1 – 9.6.3
S 9.6.4 – 9.6.5

Learning aims:

- State the conditions for rusting.

- State some common barrier methods and describe how they work.

- **S** Describe galvanising.

- **S** Explain sacrificial protection.

- Describe the ease of extraction of metals from their ores in terms of the reactivity series.

- Describe the extraction of iron in the blast furnace.

- **S** State the symbol equations for the extraction of iron.

- State that aluminium is extracted from bauxite by electrolysis.

- **S** Describe the extraction of aluminium using ionic half-equations.

Rusting

Rusting is a chemical reaction between iron, water and oxygen. The chemical name for rust is **hydrated** iron(III) oxide, Fe_2O_3. A hydrated substance is a substance that is chemically combined with water.

> **Key Point**
>
> The term hydrated was introduced as part of the preparation of salts on page 55.

Preventing rusting

One of the ways of preventing rusting involves the use of **barrier methods**:

Barrier methods	What they achieve
Painting	
Greasing	They exclude oxygen and water
Coating with plastic	

S **Galvanising** is another example of a barrier method. When iron is galvanised, it is coated with a layer of zinc. As zinc is more reactive than iron, it will oxidise more rapidly than iron and form a protective coating on the iron.

Galvanising has an advantage over the other barrier methods shown in the table.

If an iron object coated in plastic is scratched, oxygen and water will be able to reach and react with the iron. If a galvanised iron object is scratched, and the iron is exposed air and water, the zinc will react instead of the iron. This is called **sacrificial protection**. The zinc is more reactive than the iron, so it will lose electrons and form positive ions more quickly than the iron.

Extraction of metals

The most reactive metals in the reactivity series have to be extracted from their ores, which are usually oxides. Some of the least reactive metals are found as pure elements, for example, silver and gold.

The extraction of iron

Iron is extracted from its ore **haematite** (iron(III) oxide, Fe_2O_3) in a blast furnace. Limestone is the source of the calcium carbonate. Silicon dioxide is the chemical name for sand, which is found mixed with the limestone. The table summarises the stages in the process.

> **Key Point**
>
> You studied electrolysis in Section 4: Electrochemistry, on pages 42–43.

S

Stages	Reactions	Equations
1	Carbon (coke) is burnt and forms carbon dioxide.	$C + O_2 \rightarrow CO_2$
2	The carbon dioxide is reduced to carbon monoxide.	$C + CO_2 \rightarrow 2CO$
3	The iron(III) oxide is reduced by the carbon monoxide.	$Fe_2O_3 + 3CO \rightarrow 2Fe + 3CO_2$
4	Calcium carbonate is thermally decomposed to produce calcium oxide.	$CaCO_3 \rightarrow CaO + CO_2$
5	Slag is formed when calcium oxide reacts with silicon dioxide.	$CaO + SiO_2 \rightarrow CaSiO_3$

The extraction of aluminium

Aluminium is extracted from its main ore **bauxite** (aluminium oxide, Al_2O_3) by electrolysis. The process is summarised in the table.

S Extracting aluminium	Key points

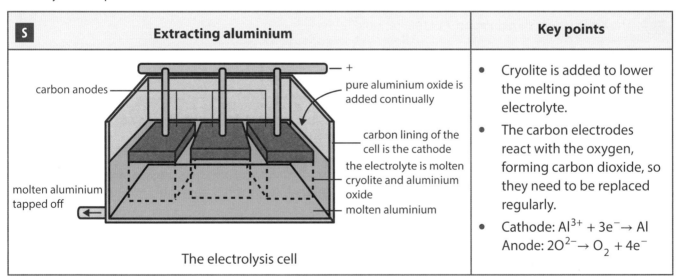

The electrolysis cell

- Cryolite is added to lower the melting point of the electrolyte.
- The carbon electrodes react with the oxygen, forming carbon dioxide, so they need to be replaced regularly.
- Cathode: $Al^{3+} + 3e^- \rightarrow Al$
  Anode: $2O^{2-} \rightarrow O_2 + 4e^-$

> **Quick Test**
>
> 1. State the conditions needed for iron to rust.
> S **2.** Describe the advantage of galvanising over a barrier method such as painting.
> 3. Name the **three** chemicals used in the blast furnace.
> 4. Name the chemical that reduces iron(III) oxide to iron in the blast furnace.
> S **5.** Describe the part played by cryolite in the electrolysis of bauxite.

Arrangement of elements

1 ▶ Nitrogen is in Group V of the Periodic Table. Select the one correct statement.

    A. As nitrogen is unreactive it does not form an ion.

    B. Nitrogen forms the ion, N^{3+}.

    C. Nitrogen forms the ion, N^{3-}.

    D. Nitrogen forms the ion, N^{5+}.   **[1]**

2 ▶ Potassium is in Group I of the Periodic Table. Select the correct electron configuration for potassium.

    A. 2,7

    B. 2,8,2

    C. 2,8,8,1

    D. 2,8,8,7   **[1]**

3 ▶ Which of these elements in Period 3 of the Periodic Table would you expect to show metallic character?

    A. The element in Group II

    B. The element in Group IV

    C. The element in Group V

    D. The element in Group VII   **[1]**

4 ▶ The table below shows Period 2 of the Periodic Table.

Group	I	II	III	IV	V	VI	VII	VIII
Element	x			y		z	q	

a   **i)** Which element has a proton number / atomic number of 6?

    .... **[1]**

    ii) Sketch an atom diagram showing the electron arrangement in this element. **[1]**

b   Which element does not form ionic bonds? **[1]**

c   **i)** Which element would have similar chemical properties to chlorine, which has an electron configuration of 2,8,7? **[1]**

    ii) Explain your answer. **[2]**

    [Total marks 6]

You may need to revise your work on Ions and ionic bonds and Simple molecules and covalent bonds covered in Section 2.

5 The table shows some of the physical properties of three Group II elements.

Element	Melting point (°C)	Boiling point (°C)	Density g/cm^3
Beryllium	1287	2469	1.85
Magnesium	650	1107	1.74
Calcium	842	1484	1.55

Identify the trend in each one of the physical properties. [3]

'Identify' means recognise and describe the trends.

Group I properties

1 Which of the following statements about potassium is **untrue**?

   A. Potassium (proton number 19) has the electron configuration of 2,8,8,1.

   B. Potassium has a lower melting point than lithium.

   C. Potassium is a soft metal and can be cut easily with a knife.

   D. Potassium reacts very slowly with water. [1]

2 Sodium reacts with water to form sodium hydroxide and hydrogen.

a **i)** Will the reaction of sodium with water be more or less rapid than that of lithium with water? [1]

   ii) Explain your answer. [1]

b Is sodium hydroxide acidic, neutral or alkaline? [1]

c Predict the pH of a solution of sodium hydroxide. [1]

'Predict' here means 'suggest a pH' – you are not expected to know the exact figure.

d Describe what you would observe in this reaction. [2]

e Write a chemical equation, including state symbols, for this reaction. [1]

[Total marks 8]

3 Rubidium (**Rb**) is another element in Group I.

Use your knowledge of lithium, sodium and potassium to make predictions about rubidium.

a **i)** What ion will rubidium form? [1]

   ii) Explain your answer. [1]

b Rubidium reacts with the oxygen in the air to form rubidium oxide (Rb_2O).

    i) Suggest how rubidium could be stored to prevent this reaction. [1]

    ii) Will rubidium oxide be an acidic or a basic oxide? Explain your answer. [2]

> Oxides are covered in Section 7. You may need to revise this.

    iii) Write a chemical equation for this reaction, including state symbols. [2]

c Rubidium oxide reacts with water to form rubidium hydroxide.

    Write a chemical equation, including state symbols, for this reaction. [2]

[Total marks 9]

Group VII properties

1 State which of the following statements about chlorine is true.

    A. It has the highest density in the group.

    B. It is a light brown gas.

    C. It is the most reactive element in Group VII.

    D. It will displace bromine from aqueous potassium bromide solution. [1]

2 State which of the following is the definition of a diatomic molecule.

    A. A compound containing a metal and a non-metal.

    B. A molecule containing two atoms covalently bonded to each other.

    C. An ionic compound containing two elements.

    D. Two atoms of the same element with different numbers of neutrons. [1]

3 This question is about bromine.

a Describe the appearance of bromine. [1]

b Describe how the density of bromine compares with that of iodine. [1]

c Fluorine is the first element in the group. Predict how the reactivity of bromine compares to that of fluorine. [1]

d Explain why bromine forms an ion with a formula of Br^-. [2]

e A solution of bromine will react with potassium iodide solution in a displacement reaction.

    i) Explain what a displacement reaction involves. [1]

    ii) State the products of this reaction. [2]

    iii) Describe what you would observe in the reaction. [2]

    iv) Write a chemical equation, including state symbols, for this reaction. [2]

[Total marks 12]

4 ▶ Chlorine reacts with sodium iodide solution. Write an ionic equation, including state symbols, for this reaction. [2]

The ions that do not change in the reaction do not need to be included in the ionic equation. The sodium ions do not change in this reaction.

Transition elements and noble gases

1 ▶ State which of the following properties is a typical characteristic of a transition metal.

    A. High density.

    B. Its compounds are usually white.

    C. It forms single positive ions.

    D. Low melting point. [1]

2 ▶ Copper forms compounds such as copper(I) oxide and copper(II) sulfate.

a State what the (I) and (II) indicate about the copper in these compounds. [1]

b Complete the table.

Name of the compound	Metal ion present	Formula of the compound	
Copper(I) oxide			[2]
Copper(II) sulfate			[2]

[Total marks 5]

3 ▶ Name the industrial process in which iron is used as a catalyst [1]

4 ▶ Copper(II) oxide reacts with dilute sulfuric acid to make the salt, copper(II) sulfate, and water. Write a chemical equation, with state symbols, for this reaction. [2]

This is an example of making a soluble salt using a base and an acid (see Section 7).

5 ▶ The symbol for argon is $^{40}_{18}$Ar.

a State the proton number of argon. [1]

b State the number of neutrons in the atom. [1]

c What is the electron configuration of argon? [1]

d Explain why argon is a very unreactive element. [1]

e Argon is monatomic. Explain what this means. [1]

[Total marks 5]

Properties of metals

1.   Which of the following is **not** a physical property of the metal sodium?

     A.   Good conductor of electricity   **C.**   High melting point

     B.   Good conductor of heat   **D.**   Low boiling point   [1]

2.   Iron is malleable. Explain what the term malleable means.   [1]

3.   Which of the following metals is used for electrical wiring in the home?

     A.   Aluminium   **C.**   Magnesium

     B.   Copper   **D.**   Zinc   [1]

4.   Sodium burns rapidly in air.

   a   Write a word equation for this reaction.   [1]

   b   Write a chemical equation, including state symbols, for this reaction.   [2]

                                                       [Total marks 3]

5.   Zinc reacts with dilute sulfuric acid.

   a   State the name of the gas produced in this reaction.   [1]

   b   Write a chemical equation, including state symbols, for this reaction.   [2]

                                                        [Total marks 3]

> The reactions of acids were included in Section 7. Some revision may be helpful.

6.   Potassium reacts rapidly with cold water.

   a   Describe what you would observe when a cube of potassium is added to the water.   [2]

   b   There are two products in this reaction. State the names of the products.   [2]

   c   The solution remaining after the reaction is complete is tested with litmus paper. Describe the result of this test.   [1]

   d   Write a chemical equation, including state symbols, for the reaction.   [2]

                                                        [Total marks 8]

7.   Magnesium reacts with steam. Write a chemical equation, including state symbols, for this reaction.   [2]

Show me

1.   Write the symbol for magnesium and the formula for water (steam). .... and ....

2.   Magnesium is oxidised by the steam and forms an ionic oxide. Check which groups of the Periodic Table magnesium and oxygen are in. Write the formula of magnesium oxide....................

3.   Hydrogen is a diatomic gas. Write the formula of hydrogen gas ....

4.   Write the equation. Check if it needs balancing. .... + ... $\rightarrow$ .... + ...

5.   Add the state symbols: (s) for solid, (g) for gas. .... + ... $\rightarrow$ .... + ...

Uses of metals, alloys and their properties

1 ▶ Describe **two** physical properties of aluminium that make it suitable for overhead electrical cables. [2]

2 ▶ Describe **two** physical properties of copper that make it suitable for electrical wiring. [2]

3 ▶ Explain why iron is not used for storing food. [2]

4 ▶ Explain which physical properties of gold make it suitable for use in jewellery. [2]

5 ▶ State which of the following is the best definition of an alloy.

    A. A compound formed by two metals.

    B. A compound formed between a metal and a non-metal.

    C. A mixture of a metal with other elements.

    D. A mixture of two metals. [1]

6 ▶ Stainless steel is an alloy.

a Which metal is the main component of stainless steel? [1]

b State **two** physical properties of stainless steel which make it suitable for making cutlery. [2]

[Total marks 3]

7 ▶ Sketch diagrams to show:

a The structure of a pure metal. [1]

b The structure of an alloy. [1]

[Total marks 2]

'Sketch' means make a simple freehand drawing showing the key features.

8 ▶ Explain in terms of their structure why alloys are harder and stronger than pure metals. [2]

Reactivity series

1 ▶ State which is the most reactive of the following metals.

    A. Calcium

    B. Iron

    C. Sodium

    D. Zinc [1]

2 ▶ State which of the following metals is below carbon in the reactivity series.

    A. Aluminium

    B. Calcium

    C. Copper

    D. Magnesium [1]

3 Look at the table. It shows if a reaction occurs in a series of experiments involving metals in the reactivity series. The metals are labelled Q, W and Z.

Element	Reaction with oxygen	Reaction with cold water	Reaction with dilute hydrochloric acid
Q	Yes	Yes	Yes
W	No	No	No
Z	Yes	No	Yes

a Arrange the metals in order of reactivity starting with the most reactive. [1]

b Complete the table by suggesting a possible name for each of the three metals.

Metals	Possible name
Q		[1]
W		[1]
Z		[1]

[Total marks 4]

4 Magnesium reacts with dilute sulfuric acid.

a Write a word equation for this reaction. [1]

b Write a symbol equation, including state symbols, for this reaction. [2]

[Total marks 3]

5 Zinc reacts with dilute hydrochloric acid.

a Write a word equation for this reaction. [1]

b Write a chemical equation, including state symbols, for the reaction. [2]

[Total marks 3]

6 Iron(III) oxide can be reduced by carbon to form iron.

a Define the term reduction. [1]

b Write a fully balanced equation, including state symbols, for this reaction. [2]

[Total marks 3]

S **7** Calcium is above zinc in the reactivity series.

a Describe what this tells you about the tendency of the two metals to form positive ions. [1]

b State which ion calcium forms. [1]

[Total marks 2]

8 Look at the equation shown below:

$$Zn(s) + 2AgNO_3(aq) \rightarrow Zn(NO_3)_2(aq) + 2Ag(s)$$

a State the name given to this type of reaction. [1]

b Deduce what the equation tells you about the relative reactivities of the two metals. [1]

'Deduce' means draw a conclusion from the information given.

c Rewrite the equation as an ionic equation without showing the nitrate ion. [2]

d Name a metal like zinc which would react with the silver nitrate solution in a similar way. [1]

[**Total marks 5**]

9 Explain why aluminium often seems to be unreactive although it is near the top of the reactivity series. [2]

Corrosion of metals and extraction of metals

1 State the chemical name for rust. [1]

2 Barrier methods are often used to prevent rusting. Painting is an example of a simple barrier method.

a Name another simple barrier method. [1]

b Describe how the barrier method prevents the iron from rusting. [2]

c Explain why iron that has been painted can still rust. [1]

[**Total marks 4**]

3 Galvanising is a process often used in the manufacture of iron objects to prevent rusting.

a State which metal is used in galvanising iron. [1]

b Galvanising involves sacrificial protection. Explain what is meant by sacrificial protection. [2]

[**Total marks 3**]

4 Most, but not all, metals are found in the ground as compounds of the metal. These compounds are often oxides of the metal.

a Name a metal that can be found in the ground as the pure metal. [1]

b Iron is found in the ground as the mineral haematite which is iron(III) oxide. State the chemical formula of iron(III) oxide. [1]

[**Total marks 2**]

5 Iron is extracted from haematite in a blast furnace. Answer the questions about the stages involved in the blast furnace.

a Coke (carbon) is added to provide heat for the furnace. State what gas is formed when the coke burns. [1]

b The coke then converts this gas into carbon monoxide. State the name of the process this conversion involves. [1]

c The carbon monoxide then converts the iron(**III**) oxide into iron. State the name of the process this conversion involves. [1]

d Describe why limestone is also added to the blast furnace. [1]

[**Total marks 4**]

6 Aluminium is extracted from a mineral called bauxite. Which of the following is the chemical name for bauxite?

A. Aluminium carbonate

B. Aluminium chloride

C. Aluminium oxide

D. Aluminium sulfate [1]

S **7** In the blast furnace, the production of iron from haematite involves a number of stages.

a Write a chemical equation, including state symbols, for the reaction between iron(**III**) oxide and carbon monoxide. [2]

b Write a chemical equation for the reaction which occurs when the limestone is heated to form calcium oxide. [2]

c Write a chemical equation for the reaction between the calcium oxide and the sand (silicon(**IV**) oxide) that is mixed with the haematite as it is mined. [2]

[**Total marks 6**]

8 Aluminium is extracted from its ore, bauxite, by electrolysis.

a Explain why cryolite is added to the bauxite in this extraction process. [1]

b State what material is used to make the anodes. [1]

c At which electrode will the aluminium be produced? [1]

d Write ionic half-equations for the reactions at the electrodes: [4]

> **Show me**

1. Aluminium is a metal in Group III of the Periodic Table. Write down the ion it forms. ....

2. To form the metal atom how many electrons does the ion need to gain or lose? Write the ionic half

   equation. ....

3. Oxygen is a non-metal in Group VI of the Periodic Table. Write down the ion it forms. ....

4. To form the element how many electrons does it need to gain or lose? Write the ionic half equation.

   ....

[Total marks 7]

Water and fertilisers

Learning aims:

Syllabus links:
10.1.1–10.1.7,
10.2.1–10.2.2

- Describe the tests for the purity and presence of water.
- State the substances that can be found in water from natural sources.
- State the beneficial substances and potentially harmful substances in natural sources of water.
- Describe the treatment of domestic water.
- State the use of commonly used fertilisers.

Water

The two chemical tests that can be used to detect the presence of water are shown in the table.

Chemical test	Observation if water present	Equation
Anhydrous copper(II) sulfate	Colour change from white to blue	$CuSO_4(s) + 5H_2O(l) \rightarrow CuSO_4.5H_2O(s)$
Anhydrous cobalt(II) chloride	Colour change from blue to pink	$CoCl_2(s) + 6H_2O(l) \rightarrow CoCl_2.6H_2O(s)$

Testing purity

The purity of a sample of water can be tested by measuring the melting point and boiling point. The table shows these properties for pure water.

Test	Result (at standard atmospheric pressure)
Melting point	0°C
Boiling point	100°C

Impurities will lower the melting point and increase the boiling point of water compared to a sample of pure water. For example, this is the situation with salt water, where salt is the impurity. In the laboratory, distilled water is used instead of tap water as it contains fewer impurities.

Impurities in water

Water from natural sources can contain several impurities. Some of these are beneficial but others are potentially harmful. The table lists some common impurities and their effects.

> **Key Point**
>
> The terms **anhydrous** (containing no water) and **hydrated** (chemically combined with water) were introduced in Oxides and preparation of salts, on pages 54–55.

Substances that may be in a natural water supply	Beneficial or potentially hazardous?
Dissolved oxygen	Beneficial for aquatic life.
Metal compounds	Beneficial – some metal compounds provide essential minerals for life, for example calcium in hard water areas. **or** Hazardous – some metal compounds are toxic.
Plastics	Hazardous – damage to aquatic life.
Sewage **and** Harmful microbes	Hazardous – contain harmful microbes which cause disease.
Nitrates from fertilisers	Hazardous – deoxygenation of water and damage to aquatic life.
Phosphates from fertilisers and detergents	

There are three main steps in the treatment of water supplies to provide water for domestic use, as shown in the table.

Water treatment stages	What the stage achieves
1. Sedimentation and filtration	Removes solids
2. Use of carbon	Removes tastes and odours
3. Chlorination	Kills microbes

Fertilisers

Chemical **salts** are used as fertilisers for crops. Ammonium salts and nitrates are commonly used as they provide the nitrogen needed for healthy plant growth.

Many fertilisers contain a mixture of the key elements for growth. The fertilisers are known as NPK fertilisers (see table).

NPK fertiliser	Element required for plant growth
N	Nitrogen
P	Phosphorus
K	Potassium

> **Key Point**
>
> Salts were included in Oxides and preparation of salts, on pages 54–55.

> **Quick Test**
>
> 1. Anhydrous cobalt(II) chloride can be used to detect the presence of water.
>   a) Explain what the term anhydrous means.
>   b) Describe the colour change when anhydrous cobalt(II) chloride is added to a liquid containing water.
> 2. Describe the major source of the nitrates and phosphates that can be found in natural water sources.
> 3. a) State the chemical formula for the salt ammonium nitrate.
>   b) Name the **two** chemicals that can be used to make ammonium nitrate.

Air quality and climate

Syllabus links:
10.3.1–10.3.6,
S 10.3.7–10.3.9

Learning aims:

- State the composition of clean, dry air.

- State the source of air pollutants and the adverse effects of these pollutants.

- State and explain strategies to reduce the effects environmental issues making use of the photosynthesis reaction.

- **S** Describe the impact of greenhouse gases.

- **S** Explain the use of catalytic converters.

Composition of air

The composition of clean, dry air is shown in the table.

Constituents of clean, dry air	Percentage composition (%)
Nitrogen	78
Oxygen	21
Carbon dioxide and noble gases	1

Pollutants and their effects

However, there are a number of pollutants that reduce the quality of the air. The table lists a few common pollutants.

Pollutants	Source of the pollutants	Adverse effects of the pollutants
Carbon dioxide	Combustion of carbon-containing fuels	Increased global warming leading to climate change
Carbon monoxide	Incomplete combustion of carbon-containing fuels	A toxic gas
Particulates	Incomplete combustion of carbon-containing fuels	An increased risk of respiratory problems and cancer
Methane	Decomposition of vegetation and waste gases from digestion in animals	Increased global warming and climate change
Oxides of nitrogen	Car engines	Acid rain, photochemical smog and respiratory problems
Sulfur dioxide	Combustion of fossil fuels containing sulfur	Acid rain

S The pollutants table shows that carbon dioxide and methane are the main sources of increased global warming and climate change. These gases are called **greenhouse gases** because they have a similar effect on the world as a greenhouse does on plants being grown in the greenhouse. The effect can be summarised as:

- the absorption, reflection and emission of thermal energy
- reducing the loss of thermal energy to space.

Reducing the effects of pollutants

Several strategies are being used to reduce the damaging effects of pollutants on the Earth's environment, as shown in the table.

Environmental effect	Actions being taken	Effect of the action
Climate change	Planting trees Reducing livestock farming Replacing fossil fuels with hydrogen and renewable sources of energy, for example wind and solar	Planting trees will reduce the levels of carbon dioxide by increasing the process of **photosynthesis**: carbon dioxide + water → glucose + oxygen (in the presence of chlorophyll and energy from light) Reduce the methane produced by livestock
Acid rain	Use of **catalytic converters** Using low-sulfur fuels Flue gas desulfurisation with calcium oxide	Catalytic converters help to reduce the levels of nitrogen oxides emitted from car engines. Using low-sulfur fuels and flue gas desulfurisation reduce the levels of sulfur dioxide released into the air.

S Photosynthesis is the process in which plants produce glucose. Importantly, in terms of global warming and climate change, it is a process that removes carbon dioxide from the atmosphere and produces oxygen:

$$6CO_2(g) + 6H_2O(l) \rightarrow C_6H_{12}O_2(s) + O_2(g)$$

In a car engine the temperature is very high when the fuel is being burnt. Under these conditions:

- carbon in the fuel can react with oxygen and form carbon monoxide, CO, and carbon dioxide, CO_2
- nitrogen in the air can react with oxygen and form nitrogen oxide, NO.

A catalytic converter catalyses the reaction between carbon monoxide and nitrogen oxide:

$$2CO(g) + 2NO(g) \rightarrow 2CO_2(g) + N_2(g)$$

This reaction removes the hazardous gases of carbon monoxide and nitrogen oxide. However, in the removal of these pollutants, carbon dioxide is formed, which is not a toxic gas but does contribute to global warming.

> ### Quick Test

1. Estimate the proportion of carbon dioxide in clean, dry air.
2. State what gas is formed in the incomplete combustion of carbon.
3. State the name of the gas that is formed from the digestion of food by animals.
4. S 4. Describe how methane, a greenhouse gas, can cause global warming.

Fuels

Syllabus links:
11.1.1, 11.3.1–11.3.7

Learning aims:

- Draw the displayed formula of a molecule showing all the atoms and bonds.

- Name the fossil fuels.

- State that hydrocarbons are compounds that contain hydrogen and carbon only and that petroleum is a mixture of hydrocarbons.

- Describe fractional distillation and the properties and use of the fractions.

Fossil fuels

The **fossil fuels** are:

- coal

- natural gas (mainly methane)

- petroleum.

Methane is a **hydrocarbon**, a molecule that only contains hydrogen and carbon. Many of the components of petroleum are also hydrocarbons. They can be represented by displayed formulae which show all the atoms and the covalent bonds. The formula shown in the diagram below is pentane.

$$H-\overset{\displaystyle H}{\underset{\displaystyle H}{C}}-\overset{\displaystyle H}{\underset{\displaystyle H}{C}}-\overset{\displaystyle H}{\underset{\displaystyle H}{C}}-\overset{\displaystyle H}{\underset{\displaystyle H}{C}}-\overset{\displaystyle H}{\underset{\displaystyle H}{C}}-H$$

> ### Key Point
>
> You will have come across displayed formulae in Simple molecules and covalent bonds on pages 16–17. A quick revision would be helpful. Displayed formulae will be used throughout Section 11.

Fractional distillation

Petroleum can be separated into its component parts using a process known as **fractional distillation**. This process is used to extract some very useful chemicals.

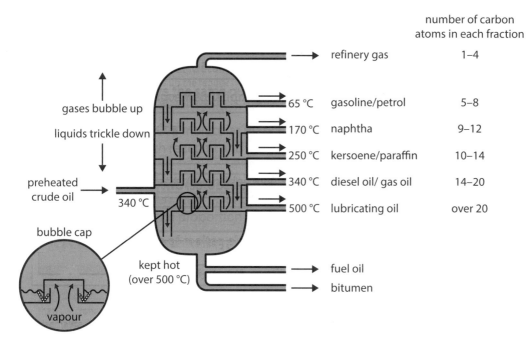

	number of carbon atoms in each fraction
refinery gas	1–4
gasoline/petrol	5–8
naphtha	9–12
kersoene/paraffin	10–14
diesel oil/ gas oil	14–20
lubricating oil	over 20

The properties of the fractions change from the bottom to the top of the fractionating column, as shown in the table.

Fractions	Properties			
Top of the column	chain length	boiling point	viscosity	volatility
↑	shorter ↑	lower ↑	lower ↑	higher ↑
Bottom of the column	longer	higher	higher	lower

The uses of the fractions are shown in the table.

Fractionating	Fraction	Use
Top of the column	Refinery gas	Heating and cooking
	Gasoline/petrol	Fuel for cars
	Naphtha	Making chemicals
↓	Kerosene/paraffin	Jet fuel
	Diesel oil / gas oil	Diesel engines
	Lubricating oil	Lubricants, waxes and polishes
	Fuel oil	Ships and home heating
Bottom of the column	Bitumen	Making roads

> **Key Point**
>
> The **chain length** indicates the number of carbon atoms linked together in the molecule. **Viscosity** is a measure of how runny a liquid is – a liquid with low viscosity will be runny and pour easily. **Volatility** is a measure of how easily a substance forms a vapour.

> **Quick Test**
>
> 1. Name the main constituent of natural gas.
> 2. Define the term hydrocarbon.
> 3. State whether a fraction obtained near the top of the fractionating column will have a short or long chain length.
> 4. Bitumen is obtained from crude oil by fractional distillation. State a use of bitumen.

Alkanes

Learning aims:

- Write and interpret the general formula of the alkane homologous series.

- S Define structural isomers as compounds with the same molecular formula but different structural formulae.

- State that alkanes are saturated compounds and have molecules in which all the carbon–carbon bonds are single bonds.

- Describe the reactions of alkanes as combustion and reaction with chlorine.

- S Describe the substitution reactions of chlorine.

Syllabus links:
11.1.2–11.1.5,
S 11.1.7–11.1.8,
11.2.1–11.2.2,
S 11.2.3, 11.4.1–11.4.2,
S 11.4.3–11.4.4

Homologous series – alkanes

Alkanes are the simplest family or **homologous series** of organic molecules. A homologous series is a family of similar organic compounds with similar chemical properties. The alkanes are **saturated** hydrocarbons, meaning that they contain carbon atoms linked together by carbon–carbon single covalent bonds. All the members of the alkane family have names that end in -ane.

Alkane	General formula C_nH_{2n+2}	Displayed formulae
Methane	$n = 1$ CH_4	
Ethane	$n = 2$ C_2H_6	
Propane	$n = 3$ C_3H_8	

S The larger alkanes can form **structural isomers**. These are molecules with the same molecular formula but different structural formulae. For example, butane can form two structural isomers:

Structural isomers of butane (C_4H_{10})

Butane

2-methylpropane

Properties of alkanes

The alkanes display a trend in physical properties, for example boiling points. They are generally unreactive organic compounds but they undergo **combustion** very readily and also undergo **substitution** reactions with chlorine.

Alkane	Combustion
Methane	$CH_4 + 2O_2 \rightarrow CO_2 + 2H_2O$
Ethane	$2C_2H_6 + 7O_2 \rightarrow 4CO_2 + 6H_2O$

S In a substitution reaction, one atom or group of atoms is replaced by another atom or group of atoms. The substitution reaction of alkanes with chlorine is a photochemical reaction: ultraviolet light provides the activation energy, E_a.

Alkane	Substitution with chlorine	Displayed formulae of substituted alkane
Methane	$CH_4 + Cl_2 \rightarrow CH_3Cl + HCl$	(structure of CH_3Cl)
Ethane	$CH_4 + Cl_2 \rightarrow C_2H_5Cl + HCl$	(structure of C_2H_5Cl)

> ## Quick Test
>
> 1. Define the term homologous series.
> 2. State the general formula for the alkane homologous series.
> 3. Write a chemical equation for the reaction of propane, C_3H_8, with oxygen.
> **S** 4. **a)** Define a substitution reaction.
>   **b)** Write a chemical equation for the reaction of propane, C_3H_8, with chlorine.

Alkenes

Learning aims:

- Write the general formula of alkenes and identify the functional group.
- State that alkenes are unsaturated hydrocarbons and describe the test that will identify alkenes.
- Describe the manufacture of alkenes and reasons for choosing this method.
- **S** Identify the structural isomers of butene.
- **S** Describe the chemical properties of alkenes.

Syllabus links:

11.1.2–11.1.3, 1.1.6,
S 11.1.7–11.1.9,
11.2.1–11.2.2,
S 11.2.3,
11.5.1–11.5.4,
S 11.5.5–11.5.6

Homologous series – alkenes

The homologous series of alkenes have a **functional group** of C=C, a carbon–carbon double bond. Alkenes are **unsaturated** hydrocarbons, meaning that one or more carbon–carbon bonds are not single bonds. Different members of the series have molecular formulae that differ by a –CH_2– unit. The names of all alkenes end in -ene.

Alkene	General formula C_nH_{2n}	Displayed formulae
Ethene	$n = 2$ C_2H_4	
Propene	$n = 3$ C_3H_6	
Butene	$n = 4$ C_4H_8	

S The larger alkenes can form **structural isomers**. These are molecules with the same molecular formula but different structural formulae.

Structural isomers of butene (C_4H_8)

But-1-ene

But-2-ene

Cracking

The fractional distillation of petroleum produces many fractions but the larger molecules in the heavy oils and bitumen amount to almost 50% of the fractions. However, smaller hydrocarbon molecules are much more useful than these larger molecules.

> **Key Point**
>
> Fractional distillation is covered in Fuels, on pages 96–97.

The manufacture of the smaller hydrocarbon molecules, such as the alkenes, is achieved by a process known as **cracking**. The conditions needed in this process are:

- high temperature
- catalyst.

For example: $C_{10}H_{22} \rightarrow C_4H_{10} + 2C_3H_6$

decane   butane propene

Properties of alkenes

As with all homologous series, the alkenes show a trend in physical properties with, for example, boiling points increasing from ethene to butene. Alkenes also have similar chemical properties.

S Alkenes undergo **addition reactions**. These are reactions in which only one product is formed. These addition reactions are shown in the table.

Addition reaction	Structural formulae of the product
Bromine or aqueous bromine	H—C—C—H (l) with Br, Br below 1,2-dibromoethane
Hydrogen in the presence of a nickel catalyst	H—C—C—H Ethane
Steam in the presence of an acid catalyst	H—C—C—OH Ethanol

The addition reaction with bromine or aqueous bromine can be used as a test to distinguish between saturated hydrocarbons (such as alkanes) and unsaturated hydrocarbons (such as alkenes). The orange solution of the bromine / aqueous bromine will be decolourised when it is added to an unsaturated hydrocarbon. This reaction can be used, for example, to distinguish between butane (no change) and butene (the bromine is decolourised).

> ### Quick Test

1. State the general formula for alkenes.
2. Define the term unsaturated hydrocarbon.
3. Describe a test that can be used to distinguish between propane and propene.

  S 4   Propene will undergo an addition reaction with hydrogen.
    a)   State the name of the catalyst used in this reaction.
    b)   Write an equation for the reaction.

Alcohols

Learning aims:

- Write the general formula of alcohols and identify the functional group.
- Describe the manufacture of ethanol and its uses.
- Give details of the combustion of ethanol.
- Draw the displayed formulae of the common alcohols.
- S Identify the structural isomers of individual alcohols.
- S Describe the advantages and disadvantages of the methods of manufacture of ethanol.

Syllabus links:
11.1.1–11.1.3,
S 11.1.7–11.1.9,
11.2.1 – 11.2.2,
S 11.2.3–11.2.4,
11.6.1–11.6.3,
S 11.6.4

Homologous series – alcohols

The alcohol homologous series contains molecules with the functional group −OH. Different members have molecular formulae that differ by a $-CH_2-$ group. The names of the alcohols end in -ol. The general formula is shown in the table.

Alcohol	General formula $C_nH_{2n+1}OH$	Displayed formulae
Methanol	$n = 1$ CH_3OH	
Ethanol	$n = 2$ C_2H_5OH	
Propanol	$n = 3$ C_3H_7OH	

S The larger alcohols can form **structural isomers**. These are molecules with the same molecular formula but different structural formulae. The structures of propanol and butanol are shown in the table.

Structural isomers of propanol		Structural isomers of butanol	
Propan-1-ol	Propan-2-ol	Butan-1-ol	Butan-2-ol

Ethanol

Ethanol is the most common alcohol. It is used as:

- a solvent
- a fuel.

Ethanol is manufactured using two very different processes. The conditions used in these processes are included in the table below.

Manufacture process	S Advantages and disadvantages
Fermentation of aqueous glucose 25 – 35°C No oxygen present Yeast as a catalyst $C_6H_{12}O_6 \rightarrow 2C_2H_5OH + 2CO_2$	**Advantages** Low energy consumption **Disadvantages** Slow process As the concentration of the ethanol increases, the yeast is less active.
Catalytic addition of steam to ethene 300°C 6000 kPa / 60 atm Acid catalyst $C_2H_4 + H_2O \rightarrow C_2H_5OH$	**Advantages** Quick process **Disadvantages** High costs due to high energy consumption and equipment needed to produce high pressure.

Properties of alcohols

As with all homologous series, the alcohols show a trend in physical properties with, for example, boiling points increasing from methanol to butanol.

There are two key chemical properties of alcohols:

- **Combustion**. Ethanol burns in oxygen forming carbon dioxide and water.

$$C_2H_5OH + 3O_2 \rightarrow 2CO_2 + 3H_2O$$

If the oxygen supply is limited, the alcohol could burn with a yellow flame caused by the production of carbon. This is the same for a Bunsen burner flame with a limited oxygen supply.

S • The formation of esters (esterification). Alcohols react with carboxylic acids to form compounds called esters.

> **Key Point**
>
> The formation of esters (esterification) is covered in further detail in Carboxylic acids, on pages 104–105.

> **Quick Test**
>
> 1. State the general formula of alcohols.
> 2. What conditions are needed in the catalytic addition of steam used to manufacture ethanol?
> 3. State which alcohol will have the highest boiling point, ethanol or butanol.
> S 4. Describe **one** disadvantage of using fermentation as a method for manufacturing ethanol.

Carboxylic acids

Learning aims:

- Write the general formula of carboxylic acids and identify the functional group.
- Describe the reactions of carboxylic acids and the names and formulae of the salts produced.
- **S** Describe the formation of ethanoic acid by the oxidation of ethanol.
- **S** Describe the formation of esters.

> **Syllabus links:**
> 11.1.1–11.1.4,
> **S** 11.1.7, 11.1.9 ,
> 11.2.1–11.2.2,
> **S** 11.2.3–11.2.4 ,
> 11.7.1,
> **S** 11.7.2–11.7.3

Homologous series – carboxylic acids

The homologous series of carboxylic acids contains molecules with the functional group $-COOH$. Different members have molecular formulae that differ by a $-CH_2-$ group. The names of the carboxylic acids end in -oic. The general formula for carboxylic acids is shown in the table.

Carboxylic acid	General formula $C_nH_{2n}COOH$	Structural formula
Ethanoic acid	$n = 1$ CH_3COOH	
Propanoic acid	$n = 2$ C_2H_5COOH	
Butanoic acid	$n = 3$ C_3H_7COOH	

S Properties of carboxylic acids

The carboxylic acids are **weak acids** as they are only partially dissociated in aqueous solution. For example, ethanoic acid dissociates as shown:

$$CH_3COOH(aq) \rightleftharpoons CH_3COO^-(aq) + H^+(aq)$$

> **Key Point**
>
> The types of reactions are the same as those you would expect with, for example, hydrochloric acid. **Salts** are formed in each case. A **base** is the oxide or hydroxide of a metal. See Section 7 on Acids, bases and salts, on pages 52–55.

> **Key Point**
>
> Strong and weak acids are covered in on page 53. You may need to revise this part of Section 7.

The reactions of carboxylic acids are summarised in the table below.

Reaction type	Example of the reaction
Metals	Ethanoic acid reacts with a metal to form a salt and hydrogen: magnesium + ethanoic acid → magnesium ethanoate + hydrogen $Mg(s) + 2CH_3COOH(aq) \rightarrow Mg(CH_3COO)_2(aq) + H_2(g)$
Bases	Ethanoic acid reacts with a base to form a salt and water: magnesium oxide + ethanoic acid → magnesium ethanoate + water $Mg(s) + 2CH_3COOH(aq) \rightarrow Mg(CH_3COO)_2(aq) + H_2O(l)$
Carbonates	Ethanoic acid reacts with a carbonate to form a salt, carbon dioxide and water: copper(II) carbonate + ethanoic acid → copper(II) ethanoate + carbon dioxide + water $CuCO_3(s) + 2CH_3COOH(aq) \rightarrow Cu(CH_3COO)_2(aq) + CO_2(g) + H_2O(l)$

Carboxylic acids also react with alcohols to form compounds called **esters**. These reactions take place in the presence of an acid catalyst. The reaction of ethanoic acid with ethanol is shown:

ethanoic acid + ethanol ⇌ ethyl ethanoate + water

Ethanoic acid can be prepared from ethanol by one of two methods:

* by **bacterial oxidation** during vinegar production
* by **oxidation** with acidified aqueous potassium manganate(VII).

Quick Test

1. State the general formula for the homologous series of carboxylic acids.
2. Define the term weak acid.
3. **a)** Write the equation for the reaction between copper(II) oxide and ethanoic acid.
   b) State the name of the organic product of this reaction.
   c) What type of chemical is this organic product?
S 4. State the type of catalyst used in the preparation of an ester.

Polymers

Learning aims:

Syllabus links:
11.8.1–11.8.5,
S **11.8.6–11.8.13**

- Define polymers and describe the example of poly(ethene) as an addition polymer.

- Describe the properties of plastics, as examples of polymers, and their environmental challenges.

- **S** Identify repeat units in addition and condensation polymers.

- **S** Describe and draw the structures of nylon and PET.

- **S** Describe the structure of proteins as natural polymers.

Addition polymers

Polymers are large molecules built up from smaller molecules called **monomers**. Poly(ethene) is a common example of an **addition polymer** and is made from just one type of monomer, ethene.

The formation and structure of poly(ethene) is shown in the diagram below. The double bond in each ethene molecule breaks and forms the single carbon–carbon bond in the polymer.

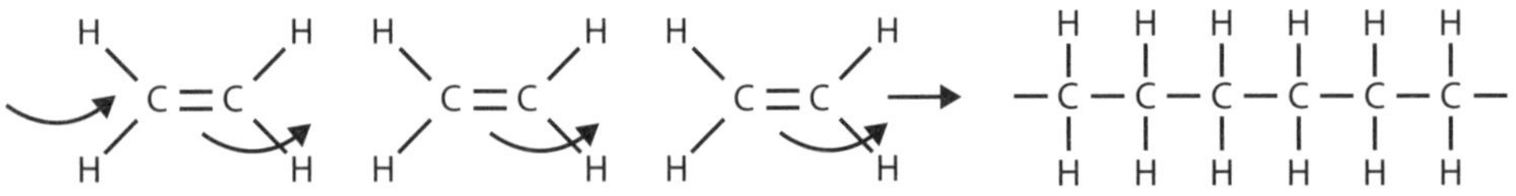

> **Key Point**
>
> Poly(ethene) is often referred to as polythene but it is important to use the full chemical name in your work.

S The repeat unit of poly(ethene) can be represented in a displayed formula as shown in the diagram below.

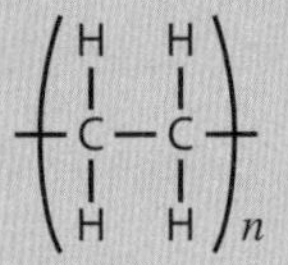

If the alkene has substituted atoms or groups the repeat unit can be identified in the same way as for ethene. For example, chloroethene on polymerisation forms poly(chloroethene), as shown in the diagram below.

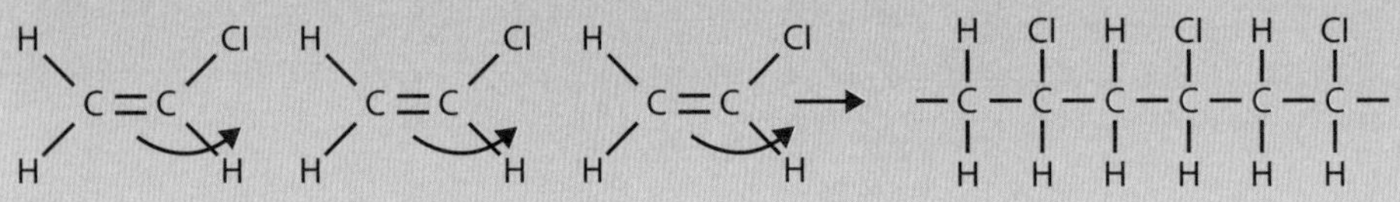

Plastics

Plastics are made from polymers. Plastics contain large molecules, many of which are very difficult to break down, which is useful for products made from plastics, but not good for the environment when these products are disposed of. **Recycling** is becoming very important in reducing the environmental implications of the use of plastics. However, challenges remain. These challenges include:

- disposal in landfill sites

- accumulation in the oceans

- formation of toxic gases on burning.

S Condensation polymers

Another type of polymer is known as a **condensation polymer**. These polymers contain more than one type of monomer. Nylon is a **polyamide** and PET is a **polyester**.

Name of condensation polymer	Monomers	Structure of the condensation polymer
Nylon, a polyamide	A dicarboxylic acid A diamine	A polyamide
PET, a polyester *Note*: There is increased use of PET as it can be converted back into monomers and then re-polymerised.	A dicarboxylic acid A diol	A polyester

Proteins are natural polyamides formed from **amino acids** as the monomers.

Protein	Amino acid (The R group can be different in different amino acids.)	Polyamide

> ## Key Point
>
> Esters were introduced in the previous topic on Carboxylic acids, on page 105. It would be worth looking back at the structures of an ester, made from a carboxylic acid and an alcohol.

> ## Quick Test
>
> 1. Define the term polymer.
> 2. Describe **three** environmental challenges provide by plastics.
> S 3. Describe the differences between addition and condensation polymers.
> S 4. State **one** advantage the polymer PET has over poly(ethene).

Water and fertilisers

1 Anhydrous copper(II) sulfate is used to detect the presence of water. State the colour change that occurs if water is detected.

    A. Blue to pink   **C.** Pink to blue

    B. Blue to white   **D.** White to blue   **[1]**

2 State which of the following does **not** present a hazard to aquatic life.

    A. Dissolved oxygen   **C.** Plastics

    B. Nitrates   **D.** Sewage   **[1]**

3 State which of the following is used as a fertiliser on farmland.

    A. Ammonium nitrate   **C.** Iron(III) oxide

    B. Calcium sulfate   **D.** Sodium chloride   **[1]**

4 **a** Describe a test you could perform to find out if a sample of water is pure.   **[1]**

    b State the result of your test.   **[1]**

                                                    [Total marks 2]

5 There are three main stages in the purification of domestic drinking water. Complete the table showing the three stages by filling in the blanks.

Stages		What the stage achieves	
1.		Removes solids	**[1]**
2.	Use of carbon		**[1]**
3.		Kills microbes	**[1]**

                                                    [Total marks 3]

6 This question is about fertilisers.

    a Phosphates are used as fertilisers. State what hazard they present to aquatic life.   **[1]**

    b NPK fertilisers contain phosphorus in phosphate compounds. State what other elements are present in NPK fertilisers.   **[2]**

                                                    [Total marks 3]

Air quality and climate

1 State the percentage of nitrogen in clean, dry air.

    A. 21%   **B.** 68%   **C.** 78%   **D.** 90%   **[1]**

2 State which of the following gases is produced by the incomplete combustion of a fossil fuel.

    A. Argon   **C.** Carbon monoxide

    B. Carbon dioxide   **D.** Oxygen   **[1]**

3 **a** State the name of the process in which plants make glucose using the energy from light. [1]

b Write a word equation for this reaction. [2]

c Name the catalyst that accelerates the reaction. [1]

[Total marks 4]

4 **a** State the names of **two** gases that are responsible for climate change. [2]

b Complete the table about actions to reduce climate change.

Actions being taken to reduce climate change		What the actions achieve	
1.	Replacing fossil fuels by using solar and wind as sources of energy.		[1]
2.			[2]
3.			[2]

[Total marks 7]

5 Nitrogen oxide is a gas that causes acid rain.

a State the name of another gas that is responsible for acid rain. [1]

b Describe how this gas gets into the atmosphere. [2]

c Explain how the production of this gas can be reduced. [2]

[Total marks 5]

6 Select the name of a greenhouse gas.

A. Chlorine   **C.** Sulfur dioxide

B. Methane   **D.** Carbon monoxide [1]

7 Describe how greenhouse gases cause global warming. [3]

The number of marks for the question indicates how many different pieces of information you need to provide. In this question you are being asked to describe three processes.

8 Nitrogen oxide forms in the engines of cars which use petrol or diesel as fuels.

a Explain how nitrogen oxide is formed. [1]

b Write a chemical equation, including state symbols, for this reaction. [2]

c Describe how the nitrogen oxide and carbon monoxide can be removed from the car exhaust. [1]

d Write a chemical equation, including state symbols, for this reaction. [2]

e State which of the products in the reaction for part d has a negative effect on the environment. [1]

[Total marks 7]

9 Plants use energy from light to make glucose. Write a chemical equation, including state symbols, for this reaction. [2]

Fuels

1 Which of the following is **not** a fossil fuel?

   A. Coal

   B. Hydrogen

   C. Natural gas

   D. Petroleum   [1]

2 Which of the following substances is a hydrocarbon?

   A. Carbon dioxide

   B. Ethane

   C. Glucose

   D. Water   [1]

3 Petroleum is a fossil fuel.

a Name the process used to separate petroleum into useful components.   [1]

b The table shows some of the physical properties of two of the useful components obtained in the above process. Put a tick in the boxes showing which component will have the **higher value** for each of the physical properties.   [4]

Component	Chain length / number of carbon atoms per molecule	Volatility / ease of forming a vapour	Boiling point	Viscosity / thickness of the liquid
Gasoline				
Fuel oil				

c Complete the table by adding a use for each of the four components shown.   [4]

Component	Use
Gasoline	
Kerosene	
Fuel oil	
Bitumen	

[Total marks 9]

Alkanes

1 What is the general formula of the homologous series of alkanes?

    A. C_nH_{2n}

    B. C_nH_n

    C. C_nH_{2n+1}

    D. C_nH_{2n+2} **[1]**

2 Which of these organic compounds is an alkane?

    A. Butane

    B. Butene

    C. Ethanol

    D. Glucose   **[1]**

3 This question is about propane.

a Propane is a saturated hydrocarbon. Explain what this means.   **[2]**

b Propane is a member of the homologous series of alkanes. Explain what is meant by a homologous series.   **[1]**

c Propane has three carbon atoms. Give the molecular formula of propane.   **[1]**

d Sketch the displayed formula of propane.   **[1]**

> Sketch means make a simple freehand drawing showing the key features, taking care over proportions.

e Propane burns in oxygen.

    i) Write the word equation for this reaction.   **[1]**

    ii) Write the chemical equation, including state symbols for this reaction.   **[2]**

               [Total marks 8]

4 Butane and 2-methylpropane are structural isomers.

Sketch the displayed formulae of these two structural isomers.   **[2]**

> **Show me**
>
> 1. How many carbon atoms are there in butane? ....
>
> 2. Butane is a hydrocarbon which only forms single covalent bonds. Sketch its displayed formula.
>
> 3. As both molecules are structural isomers, how many carbon atoms are there in 2-methypropane?
>
>   ....
>
> 4. The longest chain of carbon atoms in 2-methylpropane is the same as in propane. Sketch its displayed formula.

S 5 ▶ Ethane reacts with chlorine in a substitution reaction.

a Explain what occurs in a substitution reaction. [1]

b State the conditions required for the reaction between ethane and chlorine to take place. [1]

c Write the symbol equation for the reaction between ethane and chlorine. [2]

[Total marks 4]

Alkenes

1 ▶ What is the general formula for an alkene?

A. C_nH_{2n+1}

B. C_nH_{2n}

C. C_nH_{2n+2}

D. C_nH_n [1]

2 ▶ This question is about ethene.

a Sketch the displayed formula for ethene. [1]

b Ethene is an unsaturated hydrocarbon. Explain the meaning of the term unsaturated hydrocarbon. [2]

c i) State what reaction could be used to distinguish between ethene and ethane. [1]

ii) State what the result of this reaction would be with ethene. [1]

[Total marks 5]

3 ▶ Alkenes are manufactured by the cracking of larger alkane molecules.

a State **two** conditions needed in the cracking process. [2]

b State what manufacturing process is used to produce these larger alkane molecules. [1]

[Total marks 3]

S 4 ▶ Propene undergoes an addition reaction with steam.

a Define the term addition reaction. [1]

'Define' means give the precise meaning.

b State the reaction conditions needed in the reaction with steam. [1]

c Write a chemical equation for the reaction between propene and steam. [2]

d Sketch the displayed formula of the product in this reaction. [1]

[Total marks 5]

S 5 ▶ But-1-ene and but-2-ene are structural isomers.

a Define the term structural isomers. [1]

b Sketch and label displayed diagrams of the two structural isomers. [2]

[Total marks 3]

Alcohols

1 Which of the following substances belongs to the homologous series of alcohols?

   A. C_3H_4OH

   B. C_3H_5OH

   C. C_3H_7OH

   D. C_3H_8OH [1]

2 The table gives information about two methods of manufacturing ethanol. Complete the conditions needed for each method.

Manufacturing method	Conditions needed	
	Temperature	One more condition
Fermentation of aqueous glucose		
Addition reaction between steam and ethene		

[4]

3 State **one** use of ethanol.   [1]

4 Ethanol burns in a plentiful supply of air with a blue flame.

a Write a word equation and a chemical equation for this reaction.   [3]

> **Show me**
>
> 1. Ethanol is in the alcohol homologous series (-O-H). Write the formula of ethanol. ....
>
> 2. The blue flame indicates complete combustion. What two products will form? ....
>
>   and ....
>
> 3. Write the word equation. .... + ... → .... + ...
>
> 4. Write the chemical equation. It will need to be balanced. .... + ... → .... + ...

b In a limited supply of air, the ethanol burns with a yellow flame. Name **one** of the products of this incomplete combustion.   [1]

[Total marks 4]

S **5** The table shows the two methods of manufacturing ethanol. Complete the table by suggesting **one** advantage and **one** disadvantage for **each** method. [4]

Suggest means apply your knowledge and understanding where there are a range of valid answers.

Manufacturing method	Advantages and disadvantages	
	Advantages	**Disadvantages**
Fermentation of aqueous glucose		
Addition reaction between steam and ethene.		

Carboxylic acids

1 A carboxylic acid has the structural formula of C_3H_7COOH. Select the correct name for this carboxylic acid.

   A. Butanoic acid

   B. Ethanoic acid

   C. Methanoic acid

   D. Propanoic acid [1]

2 Ethanoic acid reacts with copper(II) oxide to form copper(II) ethanoate. What type of chemical is copper ethanoate?

   A. An acid

   B. An alkali

   C. A base

   D. A salt [1]

3 Ethanoic acid reacts with sodium carbonate.

  a Draw the displayed formula of ethanoic acid. [1]

  b Name the gas produced in this reaction. [1]

  c Write a word equation for this reaction. [2]

  d Write a symbol equation for this reaction. [2]

[Total marks 6]

S **4** Ethanoic acid is a weak acid. State which of the following statements is true.

   A. Ethanoic acid is only slightly dissociated into ions in aqueous solution.

   B. Ethanoic acid always has a pH of 6.

   C. Ethanoic acid does not form H^+ ions in aqueous solution.

   D. Ethanoic acid has no effect on damp universal indicator paper. [1]

5 Ethanoic acid reacts with ethanol to form ethyl ethanoate.

a What type of chemical is ethyl ethanoate? [1]

b Write a word equation for this reaction. [1]

c Sketch the displayed formula of ethyl ethanoate to show the structure. [2]

d Write a symbol equation for this reaction. [2]

e State the name of the type of catalyst used in this reaction. [1]

[Total marks 7]

6 Ethanoic acid is prepared from ethanol.

a Name this process. [1]

b State the name of the chemical that can be used in the laboratory to carry out this process. [1]

[Total marks 2]

Polymers

1 Which type of organic compounds are used to make addition polymers?

A. Alcohols

B. Alkanes

C. Alkenes

D. Carboxylic acids [1]

2 a Draw a displayed formula of ethene. [1]

b Draw a displayed formula showing part of the structure of poly(**ethene**). [1]

c Explain why poly(**ethene**) causes environmental problems. [2]

d State the name of a plastic which causes fewer environmental problems. [1]

[Total marks 5]

3 a Define the term condensation polymer. [1]

b State the name of the type of organic compound nylon is. [1]

c Sketch displayed formulae for the two monomers used in the manufacture of nylon. [4]

d Sketch the displayed formula showing the linkages between the monomers in nylon. [2]

[Total marks 8]

4 a Proteins are polymers. State the name given to this type of organic molecule. [1]

b State whether a protein is an addition or condensation polymer. [1]

c Proteins are made up of amino acids. Sketch the displayed formula of an amino acid. [2]

a Sketch the displayed formula of a protein. [2]

[Total marks 6]

Experimental design

Learning aims:

- Name apparatus for measurement of time, temperature, mass and volume.
- Suggest advantages and disadvantages of experimental equipment and methods.
- Describe and use a range of experimental terms.

Syllabus links:
12.1.1–12.1.3

Measuring apparatus

The measuring apparatus used in practical chemistry is summarised in the table.

Apparatus for measurement			
Time	**Temperature**	**Mass**	**Volume**
Stopwatch	Thermometer	Balance	Burette, volumetric pipette, measuring cylinder, gas syringe

> **Key Point**
>
> You will experience this apparatus in practical activities included in other sections of the course. A few examples are included in the table below.

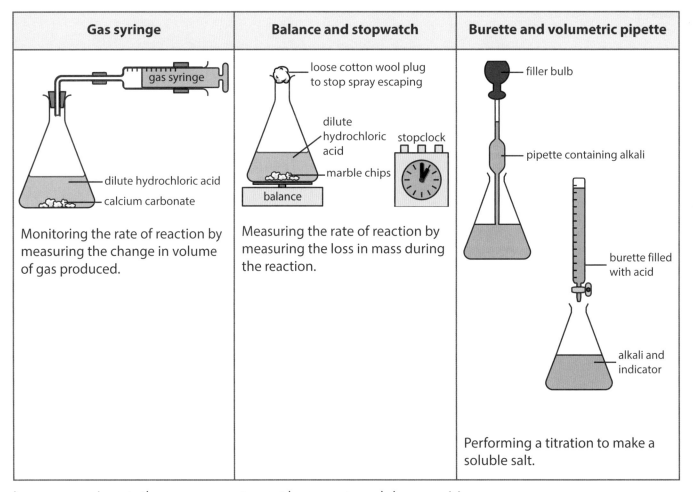

Gas syringe	Balance and stopwatch	Burette and volumetric pipette
Monitoring the rate of reaction by measuring the change in volume of gas produced.	Measuring the rate of reaction by measuring the loss in mass during the reaction.	Performing a titration to make a soluble salt.

In some experiments the measurements must be accurate and show precision. For example, a burette has the following advantages over a measuring cylinder:

- It is easier to add small volumes slowly, even a drop at a time if necessary.
- It is easier to read the scale accurately / with precision.

> **Key Point**
>
> The titration experiment is included in the next topic.

Terms used in experiments

The important chemical terms you need to be able to describe are shown in the table.

Term	Definition
Solvent	A substance that dissolves a solute.
Solute	A substance that dissolves in a solvent.
Solution	A mixture of one or more solutes dissolved in a solvent.
Saturated solution	A solution containing the maximum concentration of a solute dissolved in a solvent at a specified temperature.
Residue	A substance that remains after evaporation, distillation or filtration.
Filtrate	A liquid or solution that has passed through a filter.

> **Quick Test**

1. Sketch the apparatus that gives an accurate measurement for the following:
   a)   the volume of a gas
   b)   the volume of a liquid.
2. Look at the diagram. Label the items **X** and **Y**.

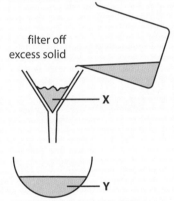

filter off
excess solid

X

Y

3. Sodium chloride is added to distilled water in a beaker at room temperature until no more will dissolve. State the name given to this type of solution.

Acid–base titrations

Syllabus links:
12.2.1–12.2.2

Learning aims:

- Describe an acid–base titration.

- Describe how to identify the end-point of a titration.

Experimental method for acid–base titrations

An acid–base titration can obtain very accurate results if the procedure is followed carefully.

1. Put on eye protection.

2. Rinse the **burette** with distilled water and then with the dilute acid you are using. Discard the solution you have used.

3. Rinse the **pipette** first with distilled water and then with the dilute alkali you are using. Discard the solution you have used.

4. Use the pipette with its **bulb-filler** to transfer exactly $25.0\,cm^3$ of the dilute alkali into a conical flask. Add three drops of indicator. Stand the conical flask on a (preferably white) tile.

5. Fill the burette with the dilute acid and make sure there are no air bubbles by the jet.

6. Take the initial volume of the acid in the burette. Add the acid to the alkali in the conical flask, swirling the flask all the time, until the **indicator** changes colour. Take the final volume of the acid.

7. Wash out the conical flask with distilled water and then repeat the titration until two readings agree to within $0.1\,cm^3$. The first titration may not be very accurate as it is difficult to know how close you are to the end-point. The indicator will change colour on the addition of one drop, so that is the level of accuracy to aim for.

The two indicators used are shown in the table.

Indicator	Colour change
Methyl orange	Red in acid → yellow in alkali
Thymolphthalein	Colourless in acid → blue in alkali

Quick Test

1. Name the item of apparatus used to measure the acid.
2. Name the item of apparatus used to measure the alkali.
3. Explain why a bulb-filler should be used in the above process.
4. Explain why the titration experiment is repeated a number of times.

Key Point

The titration method is is used in the preparation of soluble salts (see pages 54–55).

Chromatography, separation and purification

Syllabus links:
12.3.1–12.3.2,
S 12.3.3–12.3.4 ,
12.4.1–12.4.3

Learning aims:

- Describe how paper chromatography is used and interpret chromatograms.
- S Describe the use of locating agents.
- S State and use the equation for measuring R_f values.
- Describe and explain methods of separation and purification.
- Suggest suitable separation and purification techniques when given information.
- Assess the purity of substances.

Experimental method for chromatography

Paper **chromatography** is a way of identifying and separating soluble coloured substances that are mixed together.

- The sample to be identified is spotted onto a pencil line on filter paper, which is then put in a beaker containing the solvent. In the diagram below, the solvent is water.
- It is vital that the solvent level is below the ink sample. If it is not, the coloured substance will dissolve in the solvent in the beaker and will not travel up the filter paper.
- The **chromatogram** produced can then be used to identify the components of the coloured substance.

Chromatography apparatus	Chromatogram produced
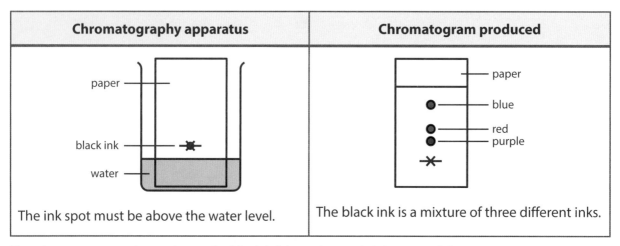	
The ink spot must be above the water level.	The black ink is a mixture of three different inks.

The chromatogram above shows the black ink is a mixture. It is impure. If the coloured substance tested was a pure substance, only one colour would show on the chromatogram.

S If the mixture contains substances that are colourless, the same procedure can be used. When the solvent has soaked up to near the top of the filter paper, the paper can be removed. It can then be sprayed with a **locating agent**, which will identify the components of the mixture.

The components can be identified by measuring the R_f value, which can be calculated using this equation:

$$R_f = \frac{\text{distance travelled by the substance}}{\text{distance travelled by the solvent}}$$

> **Key Point**
>
> Fractional distillation is an important process in the manufacture of gasoline/petrol. See the topic on Fuels, on pages 96–97.

Experimental methods for separation and purification

Method	Equipment used
Filtration – separates an insoluble solid from a liquid.	filter off excess solid / filter / evaporating dish
Crystallisation – crystals form on cooling a **saturated solution**.	transfer hot liquid to dish / crystals form after leaving to cool and when solution is saturated
Simple distillation – separates a liquid from a solution containing a dissolved solid.	cold water out / condenser / salt solution / heat / cold water in / pure water
Fractional distillation – separates different liquids from a solution / liquid mixture.	thermometer / water out / condenser / fractioning column containing glass beads / water in / almost pure ethanol / ethanol + water / electric heater

The purity of substances can be determined using two processes:

* measure the melting point
* measure the boiling point.

> **Quick Test**

1. Explain how chromatography will distinguish between pure and impure substances.
2. State the method you would use to separate sand from water.

Identification of ions and gases

Syllabus links:
12.5.1–12.5.4

Learning aims:

- Describe tests to identify anions and cations.
- Describe tests to identify gases.

An anion is a negative ion. A cation is a positive ion. They can be identified in a range of different tests.

Tests for anions

Anion	Test	Result
Carbonate, CO_3^{2-}	Add dilute acid	Test for carbon dioxide (white precipitate with limewater)
Chloride, Cl^- Bromide, Br^- Iodide, I^-	Add dilute nitric acid and silver nitrate	White precipitate Cream precipitate Yellow precipitate
Nitrate, NO_3^-	Add aluminium foil and aqueous sodium hydroxide	Test for ammonia (damp universal indicator paper turns blue)
Sulfate, SO_4^{2-}	Add dilute nitric acid and aqueous barium nitrate	White precipitate
Sulfite, SO_3^{2-}	Add acidified potassium manganate(VII)	Colour change from purple to colourless

Tests for cations in solution

The solution tests all involve using aqueous sodium hydroxide or aqueous ammonia. The result in each case is a colourful **precipitate** of a metal hydroxide, which can be used to identify the cation.

Cation	Test	Result
Aluminium, Al^{3+}	**Add:** aqueous sodium hydroxide **or** aqueous ammonia	White precipitate*
Calcium, Ca^{2+}		White precipitate
Chromium, Cr^{3+}		Green precipitate*
Copper, Cu^{2+}		Blue precipitate
Iron(II), Fe^{2+}		Green precipitate
Iron(III), Fe^{3+}		Reddish-brown precipitate
Zinc, Zn^{2+}		White precipitate*

*In these cases the precipitate dissolves in excess aqueous sodium hydroxide.

To identify the ammonium ion, NH_4^+:

- add aqueous sodium hydroxide solution and warm
- damp universal indicator paper turns blue.

Test for cations using a flame test on solids

In each test some **nichrome wire** is dipped into concentrated hydrochloric acid, then into the solid, and then into a blue Bunsen burner flame.

Cation	Colour in the flame
Lithium, Li^+	Bright red
Sodium, Na^+	Yellow/orange
Potassium, K^+	Light purple
Calcium, Ca^{2+}	Red
Barium, Ba^{2+}	Green
Copper(II), Cu^{2+}	Blue–green

> **Key Point**
>
> Limewater is a solution of calcium hydroxide.

Tests for gases

There are a number of different tests depending on the gas.

Gas	Test	Result
Ammonia, NH_3	Damp red litmus paper	Litmus paper turns blue
Carbon dioxide, CO_2	Limewater	Limewater turns cloudy
Chlorine, Cl_2	Damp litmus paper	Litmus paper bleached
Hydrogen, H_2	Lighted splint	Burns with a 'pop'
Oxygen, O_2	Glowing splint	Splint relights
Sulfur dioxide, SO_2	Acidified potassium manganate(VII)	Turns from purple to colourless

> **Quick Test**
>
> 1. Describe the test for the sulfate ion and the result of the test.
> 2. Describe how to distinguish between solutions containing Fe^{2+} and Fe^{3+} cations.
> 3. What colour is produced by K^+ ions in a flame test?

Experimental design

1 Which item of apparatus is the most accurate when measuring volume?

   A. A beaker

   B. A burette

   C. A conical flask

   D. A measuring cylinder [1]

2 Sodium hydroxide is dissolved in water to make aqueous sodium hydroxide. Which term describes the solid sodium hydroxide?

   A. Residue

   B. Solute

   C. Solution

   D. Solvent [1]

3 A precipitate has been formed by a reaction in a test tube. When the precipitate is filtered, what name is given to the liquid that passes through the filter paper?

   A. Filtrate

   B. Residue

   C. Solution

   D. Solvent [1]

4 An experiment is set up to measure the rate of reaction between magnesium and dilute hydrochloric acid. The volume of hydrogen gas produced is measured. The reaction is repeated with different masses of magnesium.

   a Name the item of apparatus that could be used to measure the volume of hydrogen produced. [1]

   b Name the item of apparatus that could be used to measure the mass of magnesium. [1]

   c Name the item of apparatus that could be used to measure the volume of dilute hydrochloric acid. [1]

   d The temperature of the hydrochloric acid must be the same in all the experiments. Name the item of apparatus that could be used to ensure a constant temperature. [1]

   e Write a word equation for the reaction between magnesium and hydrochloric acid. [1]

   f Write a chemical equation for the reaction, including state symbols. [2]

   [Total marks 7]

Acid–base titrations

1 A titration is performed between dilute hydrochloric acid and dilute sodium hydroxide.

   a 25 cm^3 of sodium hydroxide is measured. Name the item of apparatus that can measure this volume very accurately. [1]

   b Name the item of apparatus that the dilute hydrochloric acid is put in. [1]

   c 3 drops of an indicator are added to the sodium hydroxide solution. Suggest an indicator that can be used in this titration. [1]

   d The hydrochloric acid is added to the sodium hydroxide and indicator in a container that is easily swirled to mix the solutions. Name this item of apparatus. [1]

e Explain why the container containing the reacting solutions and indicator is placed on a white tile. [1]

f At the end-point, the indicator changes colour. State the colour change that occurs with the indicator you have chosen. [1]

g Explain why the first titration, often called the trial, is unlikely to give a very accurate result. [2]

h The titration is repeated another two times. The results are shown in the table.

Titration	Initial volume of acid (cm³)	Final volume of acid (cm³)	Volume of acid added (cm³)
Trial	0.0		18.5
1st accurate	18.5	35.8	
2nd accurate	0.0		17.4

Complete the missing results in the table. [3]

i Explain why, with these results, it is not necessary to repeat the titration again. [1]

j Write a word equation for the reaction. [1]

k Write a chemical equation, including state symbols, for the reaction. [2]

[Total marks 15]

Chromatography, separation and purification

1 Paper chromatography is used to investigate a sample of ink. Sketch and label the apparatus required. [5]

2 A chromatogram produced in an experiment is shown.

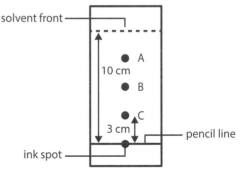

a State whether the ink is a pure or impure substance. Explain your answer. [2]

b Explain why the ink is spotted onto a pencil line. [1]

c Explain why it is important that the solvent is not allowed to soak all the way to the top of the filter paper. [1]

d State which of the components labelled A, B and C is the most soluble in the solvent. [1]

e Calculate the R_f value for component C. [2]

> **Show me**

1. How far up the paper has C soaked? ....

2. How far up the paper has the solvent soaked? ....

3. Express the distances as a ratio (as a decimal less than 1) ....

[Total marks 7]

125

S **3** Chromatography can be used to separate mixtures of substances that are colourless. Explain how this is done. [2]

4 **a** Fractional distillation can be used to separate a mixture of two liquids. State whether the first liquid collected from the condenser will have the higher or lower boiling point. [1]

b State which important industrial process uses fractional distillation. [1]

[Total marks 2]

5 **a** Explain what types of substances can be separated by filtration. [1]

b State the names of two substances that can be separated by filtration. [1]

[Total marks 2]

6 State the name of the type of solution which on cooling will form crystals. [1]

7 **a** Sketch and label a simple distillation apparatus for separating water from potassium chloride solution. [4]

'Sketch' means make a simple freehand drawing showing the key features, taking care over proportions.

b Describe how you could test the purity of the water collected by the simple distillation. [1]

[Total marks 5]

Identification of ions and gases

1 Which of the following tests is used to identify oxygen?

A. Burns with a pop.

B. Relights a glowing splint.

C. Turns damp litmus paper blue.

D. Turns damp litmus paper red. [1]

2 Dilute nitric acid and silver nitrate are added to a solution containing iodide, I^-, ions. Which of the following observations occurs?

A. A brown precipitate

B. A cream precipitate

C. A white precipitate

D. A yellow precipitate [1]

3 A flame test is used to identify calcium ions, Ca^{2+}. Which colour do these ions produce in the flame?

A. Blue-green

B. Green

C. Light purple

D. Red [1]

4 Describe the stages in performing a flame test. [3]

The number of marks is a clue to the number of stages.

5 You have been asked to confirm that a green powder is copper(II) carbonate. Complete the table showing the tests and results that would confirm the powder is copper(II) carbonate.

Ion	Test	Result of test	
Cu^{2+}			[2]
CO_3^{2-}			[2]

[Total marks 4]

6 **a** State the colour of solid sodium sulfate. [1]

b Complete the table below showing the tests and results of confirming the presence of sodium sulfate.

Ions	Test	Result	
Sodium ion, Na^+			[1]
Sulfate ion, SO_4^{2-}			[2]

[Total marks 3]

7 Complete the table showing the tests and results for detecting gases.

Gas	Test	Result	
Chlorine			[2]
	Damp red litmus paper	Litmus paper turns blue	[1]
	Acidified potassium manganate(VII)		[2]

[Total marks 5]

8 Sodium hydroxide solution can be used for detecting the presence of cations in solution.

a State the name of another solution that can be used in this test. [1]

b Define the term cation. [1]

c The table shows the results of testing for cations using sodium hydroxide solution. Complete the table.

Cation	Colour of precipitate	
Fe^{2+} (iron(II) chloride)		[1]
	Reddish brown	[1]
	Green (which dissolves in excess sodium hydroxide solution)	[1]
Al^{3+} (aluminium chloride)		[1]

d Write a word equation for the reaction of iron(II) chloride solution with sodium hydroxide solution. [1]

e Write a chemical equation, with state symbols, for the reaction of iron(II) chloride solution with sodium hydroxide solution. [2]

[Total marks 9]

9 Describe the test and the result that can be used to confirm the presence of the ammonium ion, NH_4^+. [2]

Mixed exam-style questions

1 The table provides information on potassium and oxygen.

Element	Proton number	Electron number	Electronic configuration
Potassium		19	
Oxygen	8		

a Complete the table. [4]

b Sketch a dot-and-cross diagram showing the chemical bonding in potassium oxide. [3]

'Sketch' means 'make a simple freehand drawing showing the key features, taking care over proportions'.

> **Show me**

Follow the stages:

1. Use the electron configurations of the atoms to work out the formula of potassium oxide.

2. Decide if electrons are going to be transferred (ionic bonding) or shared (covalent bonding).

3. Decide on the arrangement of the atoms so that when you add the electron shells the transfer or sharing of electrons can be shown easily in your sketch.

4. Sketch the electron shells and show how the electrons are transferred or shared between the atoms.

[Total: 7]

2 Consider the equation below:

$$CuSO_4(s) + 5H_2O \rightleftharpoons CuSO_4.5H_2O(s)$$

a Explain what the '$\rightleftharpoons$' symbol indicates in this reaction. [1]

b **i)** Name the type of compounds that include '.$n\,H_2O$' (l) in the formula (such as $CuSO_4.5H_2O$). [1]

ii) The copper(II) sulfate reactant in this reaction is *anhydrous*. Explain what this means. [1]

c State the colour of the $CuSO_4$. [1]

d Decide if the reaction is a redox reaction. Explain your answer. [2]

'Explain' means you must include evidence to support your answer.

[Total: 6]

3 Iron is a transition metal.

a List **two** properties that are characteristic of transition metals. [2]

b Iron reacts with oxygen to form iron (III) oxide. Write the symbol equation for this reaction. [2]

c Iron (III) oxide reacts with magnesium forming iron and magnesium oxide.

i) Write the symbol equation for this reaction. [2]

ii) Name the chemical that has been reduced. [1]

iii) Name the oxidising agent. [1]

d Iron can be extracted from iron ore in a blast furnace. Name **two other** reactants used in the blast furnace. [2]

[**Total: 10**]

4 Hydrochloric acid reacts with an alkali to form a salt and water.

a **i)** Hydrochloric acid is a strong acid. Explain what this means. [1]

ii) Write a symbol equation showing how the hydrochloric acid exists in aqueous solution. [2]

iii) Ethanoic acid is a weak acid. Write a symbol equation showing how ethanoic acid exists in aqueous solution. [2]

b A titration experiment is performed to determine the concentration of the hydrochloric acid solution.

i) Name the apparatus needed to measure accurately the volume of hydrochloric acid used. [1]

ii) Name the apparatus needed to measure accurately the volume of sodium hydroxide used. [1]

iii) The results of the titration are shown in the table.

Chemical	Volume used in the reaction (cm^3)	Concentration (mol/dm^3)
Hydrochloric acid	20.0	0.1
Sodium hydroxide	25.0	

Calculate the concentration of the sodium hydroxide. [5]

It is important to show all the stages of your working when doing a calculation. You can still earn marks even if you make a mistake.

> **Show me**

Step 1: Write the equation.	HCl + NaOH→ .... + ...
Step 2: Write down the number of moles of the reactants.	HCl + NaOH 1 mole ....
Step 3: Convert the moles into volumes and concentrations.	HCl + NaOH 1000 cm^3 1M ....
Step 4: Use the same scaling factor for acid and alkali. The alkali is less concentrated than 0.1M as a greater volume was needed. So the scaling factor is 20/25 × 0.1.	HCl + NaOH 1000 cm^3 0.1M+ .... 20 cm^3 0.1M + 20/25 × 0.1M = ...M [1]

[**Total: 12**]

5 The displayed formula of an organic molecule X is shown below.

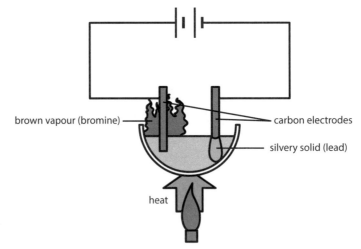

a State the molecular formula of X.   [1]

b State the name of X.   [1]

c When calcium carbonate is added to X a gas is produced.

   i)   Describe what you would observe in this reaction.   [1]

   ii) Name the gas that is produced.   [1]

   iii) Describe a test and its result that would confirm the presence of this gas.   [2]

                                                                                                [Total: 6]

S 6 This question is about the gases ethane and ethene.

a Calculate the formula masses of the two gases.   [2]

b i)   Which gas will have the greater rate of diffusion?   [1]

   ii) Explain your answer to part i) in terms of kinetic particle theory.   [1]

c i)   Which of the gases will undergo a substitution reaction with chlorine?   [1]

   ii) Write a chemical equation for the reaction.   [2]

   iii) State the reaction conditions needed for this reaction.   [1]

                                                                                                [Total: 8]

7 Lead(II) bromide is electrolysed using the apparatus shown.

brown vapour (bromine) —

— carbon electrodes

— silvery solid (lead)

heat

a Explain why the lead(II) bromide must be molten.   [1]

b i)   State the electrode at which the lead forms.   [1]

   ii) Identify whether the ions attracted to this electrode are anions or cations.   [1]

   iii) The molten lead(II) bromide is an electrolyte. Define the term 'electrolyte'.   [1]

c Bromine is in Group VII of the Periodic Table.

   i)   State the number of electrons in the outermost shell of a bromine atom.   [1]

   ii) Give the formula for the ion of bromine formed.   [1]

   iii) State which is more reactive: bromine or iodine.   [1]

d) The reaction of chlorine with aqueous sodium iodide is shown below:

$$Cl_2(g) + 2NaI(aq) \rightarrow 2NaCl(aq) + I_2(aq)$$

    i) Name this type of reaction. [1]

    ii) State whether chlorine or iodine is more reactive. Explain your answer. [2]

[Total: 10]

8   Aluminium is obtained by the electrolysis of molten aluminium oxide.

a) The ionic half-equation for the formation of the aluminium is shown below:

$$Al^{3+} + 3e^- \rightarrow Al$$

State whether this equation shows oxidation or reduction. [1]

b) Aluminium is part of a reactivity series of metals including calcium, iron and copper.

    i) Name the most reactive of these four metals. [1]

    ii) Name the least reactive of these four metals. [1]

    iii) Aluminium is less reactive than its position in the reactivity series indicates. Explain this apparent unreactivity. [1]

[Total: 4]

9   Ammonia is produced in the Haber process. The equation is given below:

$$N_2(g) + 3H_2(g) \rightleftharpoons 2NH_3(g) \; \Delta H = -ve$$

a) State whether the forward reaction is exothermic or endothermic. [1]

b) Sketch and label a reaction pathway diagram for this reaction. [2]

c) The reaction conditions are shown:

Temperature = 450°C	Pressure = 200 atm	Catalyst = iron

    i) Explain why a temperature of 450°C is used. [2]

    ii) Explain why a pressure of 200 atm is used. [2]

    iii) Explain why a catalyst is used and the effect it has on the reaction pathway diagram. [2]

[Total: 9]

10   **a)** Sodium reacts with water, producing sodium hydroxide solution and hydrogen gas. Write a symbol equation for this reaction, including state symbols. [2]

b)   **i)** Describe the test used to identify the presence of hydrogen. [1]

    ii) State the outcome of this test if hydrogen is present. [1]

c) State whether sodium hydroxide solution is an acid, an alkali, a base or an indicator. [1]

d) Methyl orange is added to the sodium hydroxide solution. State the colour of the resulting solution. [1]

e) Sodium hydroxide reacts with acids. Name this type of reaction. [1]

f) Complete the following ionic equation.

$$+ OH^- \rightarrow H_2O$$

[1]

[Total: 8]

11 **a** Complete the table showing the typical proportions of gases in the air.

Nitrogen (%)	Oxygen (%)	Carbon dioxide and noble gases (%)
		1

[2]

b Explain why the noble gases are very unreactive. [1]

c **i)** Human activities are a major source of carbon dioxide in the air. State which human activity produces the most carbon dioxide. [1]

ii) Describe a negative effect of increased carbon dioxide in the atmosphere. [1]

iii) Name a natural process that removes carbon dioxide from the atmosphere. [1]

iv) Describe what can be done to increase this natural process. [1]

[Total: 7]

S **12** When zinc reacts with nitric acid, hydrogen is produced.

The symbol equation is:

$$Zn(s) + 2HNO_3(aq) \rightarrow Zn(NO_3)_2(aq) + H_2(g)$$

In an experiment, 1.3 g of zinc is added to excess dilute nitric acid.

a Calculate the volume of hydrogen that will be formed at room temperature and pressure. [4]

> **Show me**

It is important to show all steps in the calculation.

Step 1: Write the equation	$Zn + 2HNO_3 \rightarrow Zn(NO_3)_2 + H_2$
Step 2: Write down the number of moles of zinc and hydrogen.	.... → ....
Step 3: Convert the moles into mass and gaseous volume.	.... g → 24 dm^3
Step 4: Use the scaling factor.	$\dfrac{1.3}{--}$ = ... → $24 \times \dfrac{1.3}{--}$ = ... dm^3

You will need to use the Periodic Table on page 179 for the atomic mass of zinc.

b In the experiment 0.36 dm^3 of hydrogen are collected. Calculate the percentage yield achieved in the experiment. [2]

[Total: 6]

13 You have been asked to measure the effect of temperature on the rate of reaction of magnesium and dilute sulfuric acid. You decide to do this by measuring the volume of hydrogen produced at three different temperatures.

a Sketch and label the apparatus that could be used. [3]

b State **two** conditions that must remain the same in all three experiments so that a fair test/comparison can be made. [2]

c The results of the three experiments are shown in the table.

Temperature of the dilute sulfuric acid (°C)	Time taken to collect 80 cm^3 of hydrogen (s)
25	60
35	45
45	25

i) State the effect temperature had on the rate of the reaction. [1]

ii) State at which point in each experiment the rate of the reaction would be at its greatest. Suggest a reason for this. [2]

[Total: 8]

14 Methanol, CH_3OH, is the first member of the alcohol homologous series.

In this question you will sketch dot-and-cross diagrams and displayed formula diagrams. Make sure you know the difference between the two.

a Describe **two** of the general characteristics of a homologous series. [2]

b Sketch a dot-and-cross diagram to show the electronic configuration in methanol. [2]

c Methanol burns in oxygen as shown in the equation.

$$2CH_3OH + 3O_2 \rightarrow 2CO_2 + 4H_2O$$

Calculate the enthalpy change, ΔH, in this reaction using the bond energies shown in the table.

Bond	C–H	C–O	O=O	C=O	H–O
Average bond energies (kJ/mol)	413	358	498	745	464

[5]

133

> **Show me**

1. Write the equation	$2\,CH_3OH + 3\,O_2 \rightarrow 2\,CO_2 + 4\,H_2O$	
2. Work out the energy needed to break the bonds. $\Delta H = +$ve	6 C–H = ... 2 C–O = ... 2 O–H = ... 3 O=O = ... Total = + ...	
3. Work out the energy released on forming the bonds. $\Delta H = -$ve		4 C=O = ... 8 O–H = ... Total = – ....
4. Add the two energy changes together to get ΔH for the reaction.	+ .... – .... $\Delta H =$ .... kJ/mol	

Do not forget the + and –signs.

d Propanol is another member of the alcohol homologous series. It forms two structural isomers, propan-1-ol and propan-2-ol. Sketch the displayed formulae of these two isomers. **[2]**

[Total: 11]

15 **a** The diagram shows the differences in the states of matter.

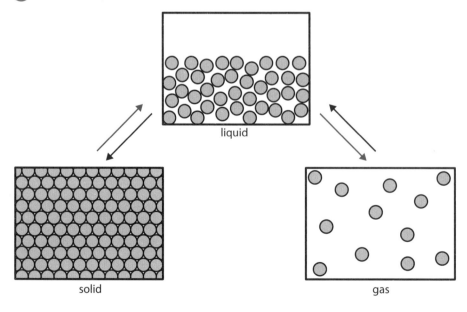

liquid

solid

gas

    i)   Name the process in which a solid turns into a liquid. [1]

    ii) Name the process in which a gas turns into a liquid. [1]

b   Use the diagram to describe the effect of increasing pressure on the volume of a gas. [1]

c   The diagram shows the structures of diamond and graphite.

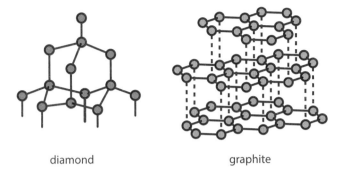

diamond   graphite

    i)   Relate the structure of diamond to its use in cutting tools. [1]

    ii) Relate the structure of graphite to its use as an electrode. [1]

'Relate' means show a connection between two things.

d   Stainless steel is an example of an alloy.

    i)   Name an element that can be mixed with iron to make stainless steel. [1]

    ii) List **two** physical properties of stainless steel that make it suitable for use in cutlery. [2]

                                                             [Total: 8]

16   The reactivity series shows the order of reactivity of metals.

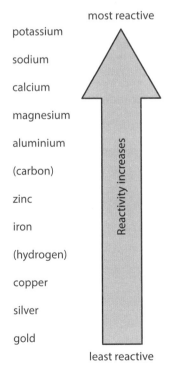

a The reactivity series contains hydrogen, although this is a non-metal. Use this information to complete the table.

Metal	Reaction with dilute hydrochloric acid. Use ✓ for a reaction and ✗ for no reaction
Iron	
Copper	
Zinc	

[3]

b Magnesium reacts with steam. Construct a symbol equation, including state symbols, for this reaction. [2]

c i) Carbon, another non-metal, is also included in the reactivity series. Write a symbol equation, including state symbols, for the reaction of carbon with lead(II) oxide. [2]

ii) This reaction is a redox reaction. Name the reducing agent in the reaction. [1]

iii) Name a metal in the reactivity series that **cannot** be manufactured by heating its oxide with carbon. [1]

[Total: 9]

S **17** The diagram below represents a polymer called PET.

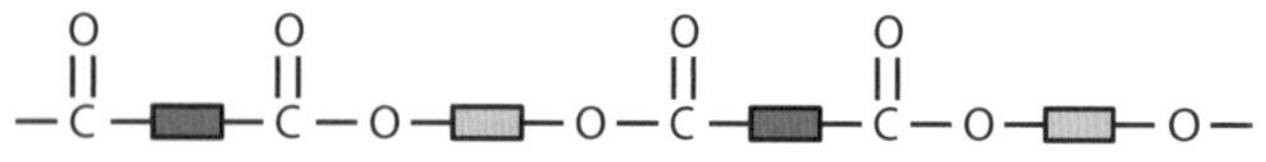

$$-\overset{O}{\overset{||}{C}}-\blacksquare-\overset{O}{\overset{||}{C}}-O-\square-O-\overset{O}{\overset{||}{C}}-\blacksquare-\overset{O}{\overset{||}{C}}-O-\square-O-$$

a What type of polymer is PET? [1]

b Plastics are made from polymers. State **one** advantage PET has compared to many other types of plastics. [1]

c Poly(ethene) is another type of polymer made from ethene.

i) Make a sketch showing how ethene molecules link to form a poly(ethene) molecule. [2]

ii) What type of polymer is poly(ethene)? [1]

d If poly(ethene) is burnt, the gases carbon monoxide and carbon dioxide may be formed. For each gas, describe an environmental problem they can cause.

Gas	Environmental problem	
Carbon monoxide		[1]
Carbon dioxide		[1]

[Total: 7]

18 Propane and propene are hydrocarbons.

a Define the term 'hydrocarbon'. [1]

'Define' means give the precise meaning.

b Propane and propene are members of different homologous series. Explain what a homologous series is. [2]

c Propane is an alkane. Propene is an alkene.

The table includes some characteristics of organic compounds. Match the statement to either alkane or alkene.

Characteristic	Alkane or alkene?	
An unsaturated hydrocarbon		[1]
General formula C_nH_{2n+2}		[1]
Undergoes a substitution reaction with chlorine		[1]
Manufactured in a process called cracking		[1]
Decolourises aqueous bromine		[1]

d Petroleum is a mixture of hydrocarbons.

i) Name the process used to separate the hydrocarbons in petroleum. [1]

ii) One of the hydrocarbons in petroleum is bitumen.

State a use of bitumen. [1]

[Total: 10]

19 Magnesium has three stable isotopes. The relative masses of the isotopes are shown in the table.

Isotope	Relative mass	Abundance (%)
$^{24}_{12}Mg$	24	79
$^{25}_{12}Mg$	25	10
$^{26}_{12}Mg$	26	11

a   Use the information in the table to calculate the relative atomic mass of magnesium.   [4]

In this calculation you can quote your answer to 3 significant figures.

> **Show me**

Relative atomic mass from ^{24}Mg	24 × 79/100 =..
Relative atomic mass from ^{25}Mg	25 × 10/100 = ...
Relative atomic mass from ^{26}Mg	26 × 11/100 = ...
Total relative atomic mass (3 significant figures)	....

b   The diagrams below show the atom arrangement in a pure metal and then in an alloy.

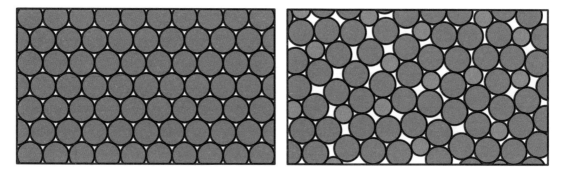

Explain in terms of structure how alloys can be harder and stronger than pure metals.   [2]

c   Iron can be protected from corrosion using barrier methods. One method is to use a coating of zinc.

   i)   Name this process.   [1]

   ii)   This is an example of sacrificial protection. Explain how sacrificial protection works.   [2]

     [Total: 9]

20 Calcium chloride and carbon dioxide are compounds with very different physical properties.

a Sketch a dot-and-cross diagram to show the bonding in calcium chloride. [2]

b Sketch a dot-and-cross diagram for carbon dioxide. [2]

To answer the questions that follow on physical properties you should include information shown in the dot-and-cross diagrams.

c Explain the following properties of calcium chloride:

  i) the high melting point [1]

  ii) the electrical conductivity. [1]

d Explain why carbon dioxide has a very low melting point. [1]

e When sodium hydroxide is added to a solution of calcium chloride, a white precipitate forms. The precipitate remains when excess sodium hydroxide is added.

Write a symbol equation for the reaction. [2]

[Total: 9]

21 The apparatus shown is used to measure the effect of changing the surface area of marble chips on the rate of reaction with dilute hydrochloric acid.

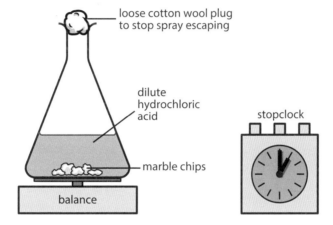

A student decides to compare the rates of reaction using three samples of marble arranged in beakers. One beaker containing large lumps, one with medium-sized lumps and one with small lumps of marble.

a To ensure that this is a fair test, list **three** conditions that must not change in the three experiments. [3]

b Describe and explain the effect of changing the surface area of the marble in this experiment. [2]

c The student measured the mass of the reaction vessel until there was no further loss in mass.

  i) Suggest what would be a suitable time interval between each mass reading. [1]

  ii) Sketch on the same graph the shape of the line for the loss in mass against time you would predict for the three experiments. On your sketch label the results with 'large' chips, 'medium chips' and 'small chips'. [3]

Decide on the labels for each axis and include units for each axis.

[Total: 9]

Instructions

- There are 40 questions on this paper. Answer **all** questions.

- For each question choose **one** of the four possible answers, A, B, C and D.

- You may use a calculator.

- You can use a copy of the Periodic Table (provided on page 179).

- The total mark for the paper is 40. The time allowed is 45 minutes.

1 Which type of substance has particles in a regular arrangement?

A. Gas

B. Liquid

C. Solid

D. Vapour

.... [1]

2 Which change of state involves a liquid changing to a gas?

A. Condensing

B. Evaporating

C. Freezing

D. Melting

.... [1]

3 Which term best describes the mixing of gases?

A. Condensation

B. Diffusion

C. Draughts

D. Evaporation

.... [1]

4 Which substance is a compound?

A. Iron

B. Methane

C. A mixture of hydrogen and oxygen

D. Sodium chloride solution

.... [1]

5 Which pair of atoms are isotopes?

    A. $^{27}_{13}Al$ and $^{70}_{31}Ga$

    B. $^{12}_{6}C$ and $^{13}_{6}C$

    C. $^{4}_{2}He$ and $^{20}_{10}Ne$

    D. $^{7}_{3}Li$ and $^{23}_{11}Na$

.... **[1]**

6 A proton has a relative mass of 1.

What is the approximate relative mass of an electron?

    A. 1/100

    B. 1

    C. 10

    D. 1/2000

.... **[1]**

7 Information about the structure of an atom is shown.

Number of protons	Number of electrons	Number of neutrons
= 19	= 19	= 20

What is the nucleon number of this atom?

    A. 19

    B. 20

    C. 38

    D. 39

.... **[1]**

8 An atom has an electron structure of 2,8,8,3.

Which group of the Periodic Table contains this element?

    A. II

    B. III

    C. VIII

    D. V

.... **[1]**

9   The calcium ion is represented by the symbol Ca^{2+}.

Which quantity of subatomic particles is correct for this ion?

A.   18 electrons

B.   22 electrons

C.   22 protons

D.   42 neutrons

.... [1]

10   Which is the correct formula for the ionic compound potassium oxide?

A.   KO

B. KO_2

C. K_2O

D. K_2O_3

.... [1]

11   Which row identifies the properties of an ionic compound?

	Melting point	Boiling point	Electrical conductivity
A.	High	High	Good when molten
B.	Low	High	Good when molten
C.	High	High	Good when solid
D.	High	Low	Good in aqueous solution

.... [1]

12   Bonds within molecules are represented by lines.

Which diagram shows the correct displayed formula for ethanol?

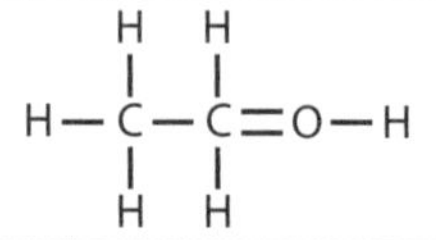

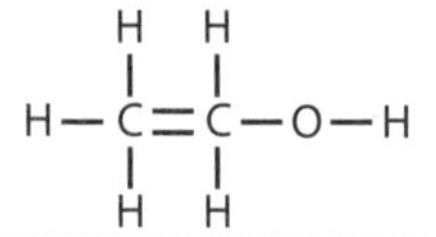

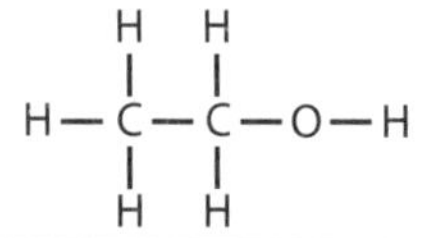

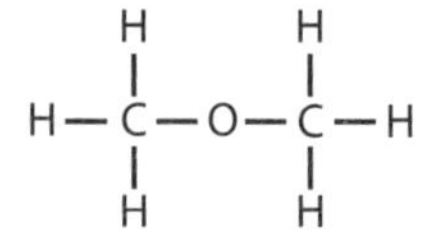

.... [1]

13 Magnesium reacts with dilute hydrochloric acid.

Which word equation, including state symbols, is correct?

A. magnesium(s) + hydrochloric acid(aq) → magnesium chloride(aq) + hydrogen(g)

B. magnesium(s) + hydrochloric acid(aq) → magnesium chloride(l) + hydrogen(g)

C. magnesium(s) + hydrochloric acid(aq) → magnesium chloride(aq) + water(l)

D. magnesium(s) + hydrochloric acid(l) → magnesium chloride(s) + water(l)

.... **[1]**

14 Use values from the Periodic Table to answer this question.

Which is the correct formula mass of ethanol, CH_3CH_2OH?

A. 26

B. 34

C. 38

D. 46

.... **[1]**

15 The diagram shows an electrical circuit used in electrolysis.

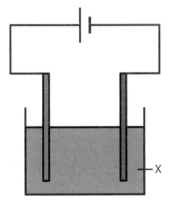

Which statement about this electrolysis circuit is correct?

A. The anions move to the electrode on the left-hand side.

B. The cations remain in the electrolyte and do not move to the electrodes.

C. The electrodes are made of lead.

D. This is the negative battery terminal.

.... **[1]**

16 The diagram shows a reaction pathway.

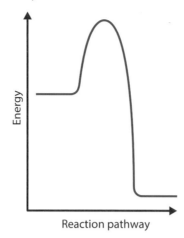

Reaction pathway

Which statement about this reaction is correct?

A. Energy is absorbed from the surroundings in the reaction.

B. The reaction is endothermic.

C. The temperature of the surroundings will increase.

D. There is no overall energy change in the reaction.

[1]

17 Calcium carbonate reacts with hydrochloric acid according to the equation:

calcium carbonate(s) + hydrochloric acid(aq) → calcium chloride(aq) + carbon dioxide(g) + water(l)

Which of these changes will increase the rate of reaction?

1. Using smaller pieces of calcium carbonate.

2. Increasing the concentration of hydrochloric acid.

3. Increasing the temperature.

A. 1 only

B. 1 and 2

C. 2 and 3

D. 1, 2 and 3

[1]

18 Which of the following statements about a catalyst is correct?

A. It changes its chemical structure during the reaction.

B. It will increase the rate of producing the product in the reaction.

C. The most common catalysts are gases.

D. The same catalyst can be used in all industrial processes.

[1]

19 The diagram shows the change in mass during the reaction between calcium carbonate and dilute hydrochloric acid.

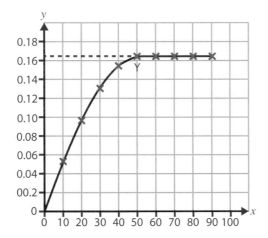

Which statements about the reaction are correct?

1. The vertical axis should be labelled 'loss in mass/g'.

2. The horizontal axis should be labelled 'time/seconds'.

3. The rate of the reaction increases as the reaction proceeds.

4. The reaction eventually stops at the point marked **Y**.

A. 1 and 2

B. 2 and 3

C. 1, 2 and 4

D. 2, 3 and 4

.... [1]

20 What observation would you expect when heating hydrated copper (II) sulfate crystals?

A. On heating, a white powder is formed.

B. On heating, the crystals form a blue powder.

C. The crystals are white before heating.

D. The crystals before heating are pink.

.... [1]

21 This equation is for a redox reaction.

$$CuO(s) + Zn(s) \rightarrow ZnO(s) + Cu(s)$$

Which substance is being reduced?

A. Cu

B. CuO

C. Zn

D. ZnO

.... [1]

22 ▶ An acid reacts with a metal.

Which substance is produced?

A. A base

B. A salt

C. An alkali

D. Carboxylic acid

.... [1]

23 ▶ The equations show possible reactions between metals and acids.

Which equations are correct?

1. $Mg + HCl \rightarrow MgCl + H_2$

2. $Mg + H_2SO_4 \rightarrow MgSO_4 + H_2$

3. $Zn + 2HNO_3 \rightarrow ZnNO_3 + H_2$

A. 1 only

B. 2 only

C. 1 and 3

D. 2 and 3

.... [1]

24 ▶ Nitric acid reacts with zinc.

Which gas is produced?

A. Hydrogen

B. Nitrogen

C. Nitrogen oxide

D. Oxygen

.... [1]

25 ▶ The table lists some compounds and their solubility in water.

Which row is correct?

	Metallic compound	Solubility in water
A.	Barium sulfate	Soluble
B.	Copper (II) nitrate	Insoluble
C.	Lead (II) chloride	Soluble
D.	Potassium sulfate	Soluble

.... [1]

26 Which of the following Group I metals is the most reactive?

A. Lithium

B. Potassium

C. Rubidium

D. Sodium

.... [1]

27 Which of these statements are properties of transition metals?

1. High densities

2. Form white compounds

3. High melting points

4. Often act as catalysts

A. 1 and 2

B. 2 and 3

C. 1, 2 and 3

D. 1, 3 and 4

.... [1]

28 Which of these properties of copper make it suitable for use in electrical cables?

1. Ductile

2. Malleable

3. Good conductor of electricity

4. Good conductor of heat

A. 1 and 2

B. 1 and 3

C. 2 and 4

D. 1, 2 and 4

.... [1]

29 Which statements about alloys are correct?

1. Alloys are produced by chemical reactions between metals.

2. Every alloy contains only two metal elements.

3. Adding impurities to a pure metal changes the physical properties of the metal.

A. 1 only

B. 1 and 2

C. 2 and 3

D. 3 only

.... [1]

30 The reactions of metals numbered 1, 2, 3 and 4 are shown in the table. Select the correct order of reactivity, starting with the most reactive metal first.

Metal	Reaction with cold water	Reaction with steam	Method of production
1.	None	Yes	Electrolysis
2.	Yes	Yes	Electrolysis
3.	None	None	Found un-combined as pure metals
4.	None	None	Heating the metal oxide with carbon

A. 1 2 3 4

B. 2 1 4 3

C. 2 4 1 3

D. 4 2 1 3

[1]

31 Iron is manufactured in a blast furnace. The table lists the stages of the process.

1.	Molten iron is removed from the furnace.
2.	Burning coke produces heat and carbon dioxide.
3.	The haematite (iron(III) oxide) is reduced to iron.
4.	The carbon dioxide is reduced to carbon monoxide.

Which is the correct order of these stages?

A. 4 3 2 1

B. 3 2 4 1

C. 2 4 3 1

D. 4 2 1 3

[1]

32 Which of the following is a physical test that can be used to test the purity of a sample of water?

A. Add anhydrous cobalt (II) chloride

B. Add anhydrous copper (II) sulfate

C. Measure the boiling point under standard atmospheric pressure

D. Measure the pH

[1]

33 Which of the following substances is beneficial in natural water sources?

A. Dissolved oxygen

B. Phosphates

C. Plastics

D. Sewage

.... [1]

34 An increase in which of these gases leads to increased global warming and climate change?

A. Carbon monoxide

B. Methane

C. Nitrogen dioxide

D. Sulfur dioxide

.... [1]

35 Which of the following organic compounds is unsaturated?

A. Propane

B. Propanoic acid

C. Propanol

D. Propene

.... [1]

36 Which of the following reactions is used to manufacture ethanol?

A. Fermentation of glucose in the presence of yeast

B. The addition of steam to ethane

C. The cracking of alkane molecules using a high temperature and a catalyst

D. The fractional distillation of crude oil

.... [1]

37 ▶ Look at the diagram of the chromatogram showing the results of testing five dyes.

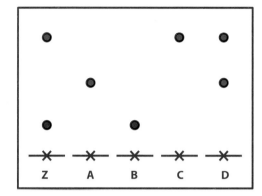

Which statement is correct?

A. B is identical to Z.

B. C is a pure substance.

C. D is identical to A.

D. Z is a pure substance.

[1]

38 ▶ Which of the following separation techniques will separate a mixture of ethanol and propanol?

A. Crystallisation

B. Distillation

C. Filtration

D. Fractional distillation

[1]

39 ▶ The table shows the results of flame tests on four metal compounds.

1.	Bright red
2.	Blue-green
3.	Yellow/ orange
4.	Green

Which of the compounds contained sodium?

A. 1

B. 2

C. 3

D. 4

[1]

40 The table shows the results of testing four metal compounds.

Metal compound	Result on adding aqueous sodium hydroxide to a solution	Result on adding dilute nitric acid and aqueous barium nitrate to a solution
W	White precipitate	No precipitate
X	Light blue precipitate	White precipitate
Y	Reddish-brown precipitate	White precipitate
Z	Light blue precipitate precipitate	No precipitate

Which of the compounds was copper (II) sulfate?

A. W

B. X

C. Y

D. Z

.... [1]

Instructions

- There are 40 questions on this paper. Answer **all** questions.

- For each question choose **one** of the four possible answers, A, B, C and D.

- You may use a calculator.

- You can use a copy of the Periodic Table (provided on page 179).

- The total mark for the paper is 40. The time allowed is 45 minutes.

1 Which of the following is the best explanation of condensation using the kinetic particle theory?

    A. As the temperature increases the particles gain energy and move further apart.

    B. As the temperature increases the particles in the vapour collide more frequently with the sides of the container causing liquid to form.

    C. On cooling the movement of the particles reduces, the particles move closer together and attractions between the particles increase.

    D. On cooling the particles move further apart and the attractions between the particles decrease as the liquid forms.

                                 .... [1]

2 Which of the following gases will diffuse most rapidly?

    A. Ammonia   **C.** Oxygen

    B. Carbon dioxide   **D.** Methane

                                   .... [1]

3 Isotopes of the same element have the same chemical properties.

Which statement is **not** correct?

    A. Isotopes have the same electronic configuration.

    B. Isotopes have the same number of electrons.

    C. Isotopes have the same number of electrons in their outer electron shell.

    D. Isotopes have the same number of neutrons.

                                 .... [1]

4 The table shows two isotopes of the same element.

Isotope	Relative atomic mass	Proportion of element
(i)	35	75%
(ii)	37	25%

What is the relative atomic mass of the element?

    A. 35.3   **B.** 35.5   **C.** 36   **D.** 36.5

                                 .... [1]

5 Which of the following dot-and-cross diagrams shows the correct ionic bonding in magnesium oxide?

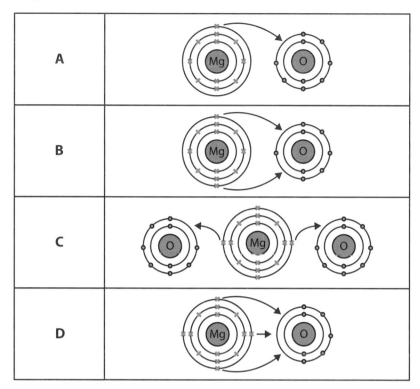

.... [1]

6 Which statement describes the bonding in hydrogen chloride?

A. A giant covalent structure containing the two atoms.

B. A shared pair of electrons between the two atoms.

C. A strong attractive force between oppositely charged ions.

D. A strong attractive force between two molecules.

.... [1]

7 Which of the following compounds contains a triple covalent bond?

A. Ethene, C_2H_4

B. Methanol, CH_3OH

C. Nitrogen, N_2

D. Oxygen, O_2

.... [1]

8 ▶ Which statements about the similarities between diamond and silicon(**IV**) oxide are true?

　　1.　They both have high melting points.

　　2.　They both have delocalised electrons in the structure.

　　3.　The atoms in both structures are held together by strong covalent bonds.

　　4.　They both have giant covalent structures.

　　A.　1 and 2

　　B.　1, 3 and 4

　　C.　2 and 4

　　D.　2, 3 and 4

.... [1]

9 ▶ What is the empirical formula of the hydrocarbon butane?

　　A.　CH

　　B.　CH_2

　　C.　C_2H_5

　　D.　C_4H_{10}

.... [1]

10 ▶ What is the equation for the reaction between calcium and oxygen?

　　A.　$Ca(s) + O_2(g) \rightarrow CaO(s)$

　　B.　$Ca(s) + O_2(g) \rightarrow 2CaO(s)$

　　C.　$2Ca(l) + O_2(g) \rightarrow 2CaO(s)$

　　D.　$2Ca(s) + O_2(g) \rightarrow 2CaO(s)$

.... [1]

11 ▶ What is the ionic equation for the reaction between copper (**II**) sulfate solution and aqueous sodium hydroxide?

　　A.　$Cu^{2+}(aq) + OH^{2-}(aq) \rightarrow CuOH(s)$

　　B.　$Cu^{2+}(aq) + 2OH^-(aq) \rightarrow Cu(OH)_2(aq)$

　　C.　$Cu^{2+}(aq) + 2OH^-(aq) \rightarrow Cu(OH)_2(s)$

　　D.　$2Cu^{2+}(aq) + 2OH^-(aq) \rightarrow Cu(OH)_2(s)$

.... [1]

12 ▶ What is the molar mass of ethene, C_2H_4?

　　A.　14g

　　B.　16g

　　C.　28g

　　D.　32g

.... [1]

13 Magnesium reacts with oxygen:

$$2\,Mg(s) + O_2(g) \rightarrow 2MgO(s)$$

What mass of magnesium oxide can be made from 6 g of magnesium?

A. 6.7 g

B. 8 g

C. 10 g

D. 12 g

.... [1]

14 Hydrogen reacts with oxygen to form water:

$$2H_2(g) + O_2(g) \rightarrow 2H_2O(l)$$

What volume of hydrogen at r.t.p. is needed to produce 18 g of water?

A. $6\,dm^3$

B. $12\,dm^3$

C. $24\,dm^3$

D. $46\,dm^3$

.... [1]

15 In a titration between $25\,cm^3$ of $0.1\,mol/dm^3$ sodium hydroxide and hydrochloric acid, the end point is reached when $20\,cm^3$ of hydrochloric acid has been added.

This is the equation for the reaction:

$$HCl(aq) + NaOH(aq) \rightarrow NaCl(aq) + H_2O(l)$$

What is the concentration of the hydrochloric acid?

A. $0.08\,mol/dm^3$

B. $0.1\,mol/dm$

C. $0.125\,mol/dm^3$

D. $0.2\,mol/dm^3$

.... [1]

16 Magnesium reacts with sulfuric acid:

$$Mg(s) + H_2SO_4(aq) \rightarrow MgSO_4(aq) + H_2(g)$$

When 4 g of magnesium are used, $2\,dm^3$ of hydrogen are collected at r.t.p. What is the percentage yield in this reaction?

A. 25%

B. 50%

C. 75%

D. 100%

.... [1]

17 A hydrocarbon contains 6 g of carbon and 1.5 g of hydrogen.

What is the empirical formula of the hydrocarbon?

A. CH_3

B. CH_4

C. C_2H_4

D. C_2H_6

[1]

18 The electrical circuit shown in the diagram is used to demonstrate electrolysis.

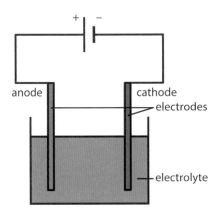

Which of the following statements is **not** correct?

A. Anions are discharged at the anode.

B. Electrons flow in the external circuit from the cathode to the anode.

C. Positive ions are discharged at the cathode.

D. The ions in the electrolyte are free to move towards the electrodes.

[1]

19 Copper (II) sulfate solution is electrolysed using copper electrodes. Which of the following statements is true?

A. Copper ions are discharged at the anode.

B. Oxygen is formed at the cathode.

C. The concentration of Cu^{2+} ions in the electrolyte decreases.

D. The mass of the cathode increases due to the formation of copper.

[1]

20 The diagram shows the electrolysis of very dilute sodium chloride solution.

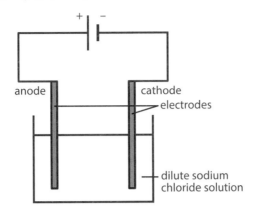

What is the ionic half-equation for the reaction at the anode?

A. $2Cl^-(aq) \rightarrow Cl_2(g) + 2e^-$

B. $2H^+(aq) + 2e^- \rightarrow H_2(g)$

C. $4OH^-(aq) \rightarrow 2H_2O(l) + O_2(g) + 4e^-$

D. $Na^+(aq) + e^- \rightarrow Na(s)$

.... [1]

21 The diagram shows a reaction pathway diagram for a reaction.

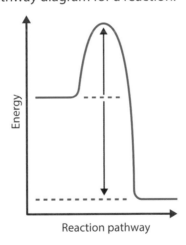

Which of the following statements are correct?

1. The activation energy is greater than the enthalpy change of the reaction.

2. The reaction is exothermic.

3. The enthalpy change, ΔH, is negative.

4. Thermal energy is transferred to the surroundings in the reaction.

A. 1 and 2

B. 1, 3 and 4

C. 2, 3 and 4

D. 3 and 4

.... [1]

22 Methane reacts with oxygen:

$$CH_4(g) + 2O_2(g) \rightarrow CO_2(g) + 2H_2O(l)$$

The table gives the relevant bond energies.

Bond	C–H	O=O	C=O	H–O
Bond energy kJ/mol	413	498	745	464

What is the correct calculation to determine the enthalpy change of the reaction?

A. $\Delta H = (2 \times 413) + (1 \times 498) + (2 \times 745) + (4 \times 464) = 4670$ kJ

B. $\Delta H = (4 \times 413) + (2 \times 498) + (2 \times 745) + (4 \times 464) = 599 \, 4$kJ

C. $\Delta H = (4 \times 413) + (2 \times 498) + (2 \times 745) - (4 \times 464) = 2282$ kJ

D. $\Delta H = (4 \times 413) + (2 \times 498) - (2 \times 745) - (4 \times 464) = -698$ kJ

.... [1]

23 A catalyst increases the rate of a reaction.

Which is the correct explanation for this?

A. A catalyst breaks down during the reaction, increasing its surface area.

B. A catalyst decreases the activation energy of the reaction.

C. A catalyst increases the pressure affecting the reaction.

D. A catalyst increases the temperature of the reaction.

.... [1]

24 Nitrogen and hydrogen react to form ammonia:

$$N_2(g) + 3H_2(g) \rightleftharpoons 2NH_3(g) \, \Delta H = -ve$$

Which change in conditions could increase the amount of ammonia produced once an equilibrium position has been reached?

A. Adding a catalyst.

B. Increasing the pressure of the reaction.

C. Increasing the temperature of the reaction.

D. Reducing the volume of nitrogen used.

.... [1]

25 The Contact process is used to produce sulfuric acid.

One stage of this process is the production of sulfur trioxide gas:

$$2SO_2(g) + O_2(g) \rightleftharpoons 2SO_3(g) \, \Delta H = -ve$$

Which row describes the best conditions for this reaction?

	Temperature (°C)	Pressure (kPa)	Catalyst
A.	450	20 000	Iron
B.	200	20 000	Nickel
C.	800	200	Vanadium(V) oxide
D.	450	200	Vanadium(V) oxide

.... [1]

26 The following equation shows a redox reaction:

$$3\,Mg(s) + Fe_2O_3(s) \rightarrow 2Fe(s) + 3MgO(s)$$

Which of the following statements describe this reaction?

1. The magnesium has been oxidised.
2. The oxidation state of the magnesium has increased in the reaction.
3. The oxidation state of the iron has increased in the reaction.
4. The iron has gained electrons in the reaction.

A. 1 and 2

B. 1 and 3

C. 1, 2 and 4

D. 2, 3 and 4

.... [1]

27 Which of the following statements is **not** correct?

A. A base is a proton acceptor.

B. An acid is a proton donor.

C. Ethanoic acid is a strong acid.

D. Hydrochloric acid solution is fully dissociated into ions.

.... [1]

28 Which of the following is an amphoteric oxide?

A. Al_2O_3

B. CuO

C. Fe_2O_3

D. Na_2O

.... [1]

29 ▶ Which of the following statements about cobalt chloride crystals are true?

1. The crystals are hydrated.

2. The crystals contain water of crystallisation.

3. On heating, the crystals change colour from pink to blue.

4. The crystals have the formula $CoCl_2.5H_2O$.

A. 1 and 2

B. 2 and 4

C. 1, 2 and 3

D. 1, 3 and 4

.... [1]

30 ▶ The table lists the stages for preparing an insoluble salt by precipitation.

Stage	Procedure
1	Mix the two solutions
2	Leave to dry
3	Wash the precipitate with a little water
4	Filter the mixture to separate the precipitate

Which row below shows the correct order for this process?

A.	1 2 4 3
B.	1 4 2 3
C.	1 3 4 2
D.	1 4 3 2

.... [1]

31 A student places a sample of aluminium in water at room temperature.

Which row of the table gives the most likely observation and explanation?

	Observation	Explanation
A.	No reaction	Surface of aluminium is coated with an oxide layer, which prevents water from reaching the metal
B.	Slow reaction	Aluminium is more reactive than magnesium
C.	Very violent reaction, gas produced and sample catches fire	Aluminium is more reactive than sodium
D.	Violent reaction, gas produced but sample does not catch fire	Aluminium is more reactive than calcium

.... [1]

32 Coating iron with zinc prevents corrosion. Which of the following statements is **not** true?

A. It is an example of a barrier method.

B. It is an example of sacrificial protection.

C. Zinc is less reactive than iron.

D. Zinc will protect the iron even if the zinc coating is scratched.

.... [1]

33 Which of the following gases is removed from car exhaust gases by a catalytic converter?

A. Carbon dioxide

B. Nitrogen

C. Nitrogen oxide

D. Sulfur dioxide

.... [1]

34 Which statements are characteristics of a homologous series?

1. The compounds have the same boiling point.

2. The compounds have the same functional group.

3. The compounds differ from one member to the next by a $-CH_2-$ unit.

4. The compounds have the same general formula.

A. 1 and 2

B. 2 and 4

C. 1, 2 and 3

D. 2, 3 and 4

.... [1]

35 Which of the following is the correct structural formula of butanol?

A.	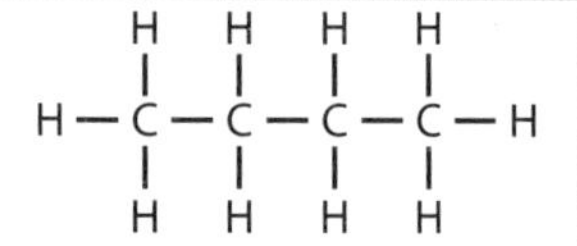 H—C—C—C—C—H (all single bonds, all H)
B.	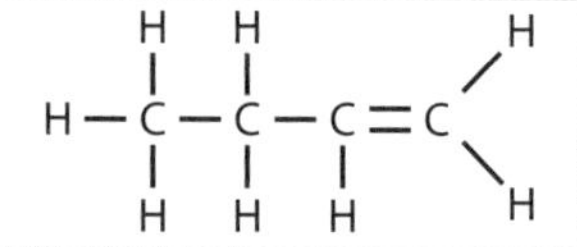 H—C—C—C=C (with H atoms)
C.	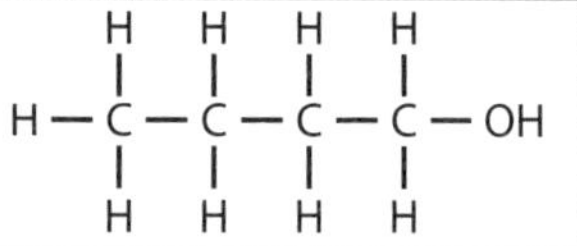 H—C—C—C—C—OH (all single bonds, all H)
D.	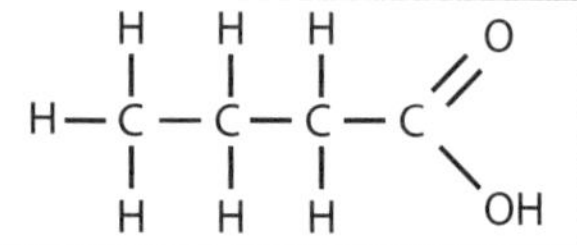 H—C—C—C—C with =O and OH

.... [1]

36 Which of the following are structural isomers?

1.	H—C—C—C—C—H (all single bonds, all H)
2.	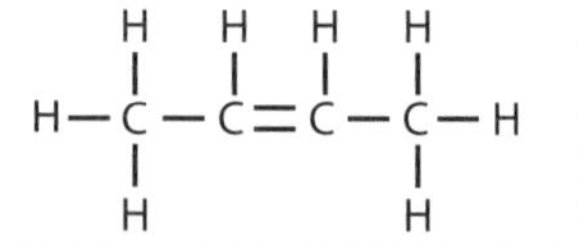 H—C—C=C—C—H (with H atoms)
3.	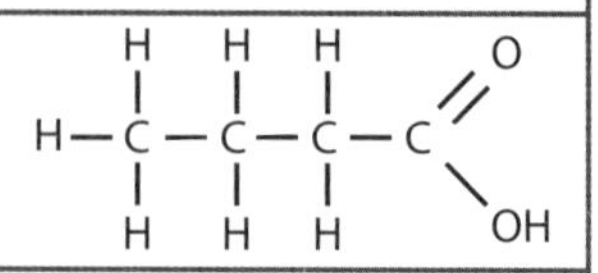 H—C—C—C—C with =O and OH
4.	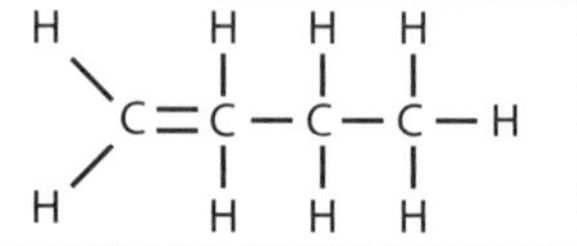 C=C—C—C—H (with H atoms)

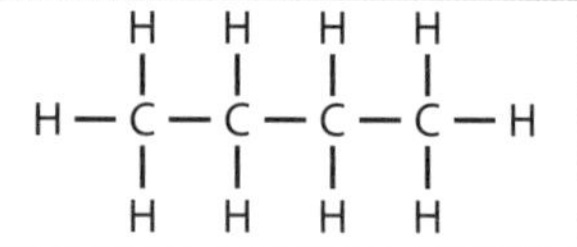

A. 1 and 2   **C.** 2 and 4

B. 1 and 3   **D.** 3 and 4

.... [1]

37 Ethane will undergo a substitution reaction with chlorine.

$$C_2H_6 + Cl_2 \rightarrow C_2H_5Cl + HCl$$

What are the correct reaction conditions?

A. Acid catalyst

B. Iron catalyst

C. Temperature of 200°C

D. Ultraviolet light

.... [1]

38 An alcohol will react with a carboxylic acid.

Which statement about this reaction is correct?

A. A salt is formed.

B. An ester is formed.

C. It is a neutralisation reaction.

D. It is an addition reaction.

.... [1]

39 The diagram shows a polymer.

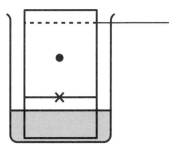

What type of polymer is shown?

A. A polyamide

B. A polyester

C. A protein

D. An addition polymer

.... [1]

40 A chromatogram shows the movement of the dye in a sample of ink. What is the R_f value for the dye?

A. 0.5

B. 0.8

C. 5.0

D. 6.0

.... [1]

Instructions

- Answer **all** questions.
- Write your answer to each question in the space provided.
- You may use a calculator.
- You can use a copy of the Periodic Table (provided on page 179).
- The total mark for the paper is 80. The time allowed is 1 hour and 15 minutes.

1 **a** Sketch the arrangements of particles in **(i)** a liquid and **(ii)** a gas. Use the boxes provided.

Liquid	Gas

[2]

b Name the process involved in the change of state from:

i) liquid to gas

.... [1]

ii) gas to liquid.

.... [1]

c The process of diffusion is more rapid in gases than in liquids. Explain this in terms of kinetic particle theory.

.... [1]

[Total: 5]

2 **a** Complete the table to show the relative charges and masses of the particles.

Type of particle	Relative mass	Relative charge
Proton	1	
Neutron		0
Electron	1/2000	

[3]

b The structure of a sodium atom is represented by $^{23}_{11}\text{Na}$.

i) State the number of protons in an atom of sodium.

.... [1]

ii) State the number of neutrons in an atom of sodium.

.... [1]

iii) Deduce the electronic configuration in an atom of sodium.

Use the Periodic Table to help you.

.... [1]

iv) Deduce the electronic configuration of a sodium ion.

.... [1]

[Total: 7]

3 **a** Sketch a dot-and-cross diagram to show the covalent bonds in a molecule of water.

[2]

b Explain in terms of the bonding in water why it shows very poor electrical conductivity.

....

.... [2]

[Total: 4]

4 Calcium burns in the air to form calcium oxide, a white powder.

a Complete the word equation for this reaction.

calcium + ... → calcium oxide [1]

b Complete the symbol equation, including state symbols, for this reaction.

.... $Ca(s) +$ .... $(g) → 2CaO(s)$ [2]

c Calcium oxide reacts with dilute hydrochloric acid to form calcium chloride and water.

For questions (i) and (ii), choose the correct term from the list:

acid   alkali   base   indicator   salt

i) State the general term used to describe metal oxides such as calcium oxide.

.... [1]

ii) State the general term used to describe compounds (such as calcium chloride) that are formed in a reaction between a metal oxide and an acid.

.... [1]

d Use the Periodic Table to calculate the relative formula mass of calcium oxide.

.... [1]

[Total: 6]

5 The table shows the products formed during the electrolysis of three electrolytes.

a Complete the table showing the missing products.

Electrolyte	Product at the anode	Product at the cathode
Molten lead(II) bromide	Bromine	
Dilute sulfuric acid		Hydrogen
Molten aluminium oxide		Aluminium

[3]

b During electrolysis of these electrolytes it is important that the electrodes are inert (do not react) during the process. Name a substance that could be used to provide an inert electrode.

.... [1]

c Electrolysis can be used to electroplate a metal. Give a reason why some metal objects are electroplated.

.... [1]

[Total: 5]

6 A reaction pathway diagram is shown.

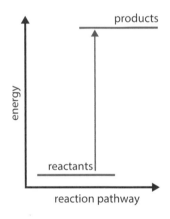

a What will happen to the temperature of the surroundings in this reaction?

.... [1]

b Name this type of reaction.

.... [1]

[Total: 2]

7 Calcium carbonate reacts with dilute hydrochloric acid.

The diagram shows the apparatus used to measure the effect of concentration on the rate of this reaction.

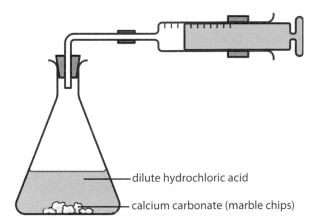

dilute hydrochloric acid

calcium carbonate (marble chips)

A student repeats the experiment using three different concentrations of dilute hydrochloric acid.

a Name the apparatus used to collect the gas produced in the reaction.

.... **[1]**

b The student performed three experiments.

i) Name two of the reaction conditions that should **not** change in the three experiments.

....

.... **[2]**

ii) Name one of the reaction conditions that should change.

.... **[1]**

c In each experiment, the student measures the volume of gas produced every 10 seconds until the reaction stops. In the third experiment, the reaction stopped after 60 seconds with 90 cm^3 of gas produced.

i) Sketch a graph, with labelled axes, showing the change in volume against time in this third experiment.

[2]

ii) At what stage of the reaction is the rate of reaction greatest? Explain your answer.

....

.... **[2]**

[Total: 8]

8 Magnesium reacts with copper (II) oxide:

$$Mg + CuO \rightarrow MgO + Cu$$

a State the oxidation number of copper in CuO.

.... [1]

b Name the reactant that is oxidised in the reaction.

.... [1]

c This reaction involves both oxidation and reduction. Name this type of reaction.

.... [1]

[Total: 3]

9 Four solutions are tested using universal indicator paper. The results are shown in the table.

Solution	Universal indicator, pH
X	13
Y	7
Z	9
W	3

a Identify the neutral solution.

.... [1]

b Identify the strong alkali.

.... [1]

c Solution W is tested with methyl orange indicator.

State what colour would be shown by the indicator.

.... [1]

d Complete the ionic equation below showing the neutralisation reaction between an acid and an alkali.

.... (aq) + ... (aq) $\rightarrow$ H$_2$O(l)   [2]

[Total: 5]

10 Copper(II) sulfate is a soluble salt and can be prepared by adding copper(II) carbonate powder to dilute sulfuric acid.

a Describe how crystals of copper(II) sulfate can be prepared using this reaction. You should describe each of the stages of the preparation.

....

....

....

....

....

[5]

b Copper(II) sulfate crystals contain water that is chemically combined with the copper(II) sulfate. State the name that is used to describe such crystals that contain water.

....

[1]

[Total: 6]

11 The Periodic Table contains the metals lithium, sodium and potassium.

a Explain why these three metals have similar:

i) physical properties

....

[1]

ii) chemical properties.

....

[1]

b State the charge on the potassium ion.

....

[1]

c State which is the most reactive of the three metals.

....

[1]

d The compound potassium chloride is tested in a flame test.

i) Describe how to perform a flame test.

....

....

[2]

ii) State the colour of the flame in this flame test.

....

[1]

[Total: 7]

12 Noble gases are elements in Group VIII.

a The noble gases are monatomic. Explain what this means.

....

[1]

b Explain why the noble gases are inert.

....

....

[2]

[Total: 3]

13 Metals can be arranged in order of reactivity.

This reactivity series includes calcium, copper, iron and magnesium.

a State which of the four metals is the most reactive.

....

[1]

b State which of the four metals is the least reactive.

.... [1]

c Magnesium reacts with steam.

i) Write a word equation for this reaction.

.... [1]

ii) Write a symbol equation, including state symbols, for this reaction.

.... [2]

d Iron rusts in the presence of oxygen and water. It can be protected by barrier methods. List **two** common barrier methods.

....

.... [2]

[Total: 7]

14 The table shows some of the substances found in natural water supplies.

Dissolved oxygen	Metal compounds	Plastics	Sewage	Nitrates	Phosphates

a State **one** source of nitrates.

.... [1]

b State **one** source of phosphates.

.... [1]

c Describe a negative impact that nitrates and phosphates have on a river or stream.

.... [1]

[Total: 3]

15 Petroleum is a mixture of hydrocarbons.

a Define the term hydrocarbon.

.... [1]

b Name the process in which petroleum is separated into its constituent hydrocarbons.

.... [1]

c One of the gases responsible for global warming is a hydrocarbon.

i) Name this hydrocarbon.

.... [1]

ii) Sketch the displayed formula of this hydrocarbon.

[1]

d Ethene is an example of an unsaturated hydrocarbon.

i) Sketch the displayed formula for ethene.

[1]

ii) Alkenes such as ethene can be obtained from saturated hydrocarbons by an industrial process. Name this industrial process.

.... [1]

iii) Complete the table to describe the test that distinguishes between saturated and unsaturated hydrocarbons.

Test	Result for unsaturated hydrocarbon

[2]

iv) Ethene is used to make the polymer, poly(ethene). Name this type of polymerisation.

.... [1]

[Total: 9]

Instructions

- Answer **all** questions.
- Write your answer to each question in the space provided.
- You may use a calculator.
- You can use a copy of the Periodic Table (provided on page 179).
- The total mark for the paper is 80. The time allowed is 1 hour and 15 minutes.

1 **a** The table shows conditions that change the volume of a gas. Complete the table.

Change made to a gas	Effect on the volume of the gas	Explanation for the change using kinetic particle theory
Increase in temperature		
Increase in pressure		

[4]

b The diagram below shows a reaction pathway diagram for the reaction between sodium and water.

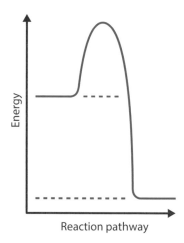

On the diagram label the following:

i) The enthalpy change in the reaction, ΔH. [1]

ii) The activation energy. [1]

c Deduce whether the reaction is exothermic or endothermic.

.... [1]

d A gas is formed in the reaction which burns with a pop when in contact with air. Write a chemical equation, including state symbols, for this reaction.

.... [2]

[Total: 9]

2 Aluminium is a metal in Group III of the Periodic Table.

a Use the Periodic Table to work out the electron configuration of aluminium.

.... [1]

b Use the Periodic Table to deduce the charge on an aluminium ion.

.... [1]

c Aluminium forms the oxide, aluminium oxide.

   i) State the formula of aluminium oxide.

.... [1]

   ii) Work out the formula mass of aluminium oxide.

.... [1]

   iii) Work out the mass of 0.1 mol of aluminium oxide.

.... [1]

   iv) Write a chemical equation, with state symbols, for the reaction of aluminium with oxygen.

....

.... [2]

d Aluminium chloride has the formula $AlCl_3$. Sketch a dot-and-cross diagram showing the formation of ionic bonds in aluminium chloride.

[2]

e Aluminium is extracted from the mineral bauxite in an industrial process during electrolysis.

   i) Give the chemical name for bauxite.

.... [1]

   ii) Cryolite is added to the molten electrolyte. Explain the function/role of the cryolite.

.... [1]

   iii) The carbon anodes must be replaced regularly. Explain the reason for this.

.... [1]

   iv) Write an ionic half-equation for the reaction at the cathode.

.... [2]

[Total:14]

3 Methanol is the first member of the alcohol homologous series.

a Describe **two** general characteristics of a homologous series.

....

.... [2]

b Sketch a dot-and-cross diagram showing the electronic configuration of methanol.

[2]

c Explain why methanol has a low boiling point.

.... [1]

d Methanol burns in oxygen forming carbon dioxide and water. Write a symbol equation for the reaction.

.... [2]

e Another alcohol is propanol. Propanol has two structural isomers, propan-1-ol and propan-2-ol. Sketch these structural isomers.

Propan-1-ol	Propan-2-ol

[2]

[Total: 9]

4 The apparatus shown is used in the electrolysis of dilute sodium bromide solution.

a State the formulae of the ions present in dilute sodium bromide solution.

....

.... [2]

b Write an ionic half-equation for the reaction at the anode.

.... [2]

c Write an ionic half-equation for the reaction at the cathode.

.... [2]

d Predict how the products of the electrolysis would be different if concentrated sodium bromide solution was used.

.... [1]

[Total: 7]

5 Ammonia is prepared in industry by the Haber process as shown in the equation:

$$N_2(g) + 3H_2(g) \rightleftharpoons 2NH_3(g)$$

a Describe what is happening when an equilibrium is reached in this reaction.

....

.... [1]

b i) Name the catalyst used to increase the rate of the reaction.

.... [1]

ii) Explain how a catalyst increases the rate of the reaction.

.... [1]

iii) Describe a chemical test that can be used to detect the presence of ammonia.

.... [1]

c i) Name **two** greenhouse gases.

....

.... [2]

ii) Describe how these gases lead to global warming.

....

.... [2]

d Catalytic converters remove the oxides of nitrogen formed in car engines. How are the oxides of nitrogen formed?

.... [1]

[Total: 9]

6 Copper(II) hydroxide can be prepared in a precipitation reaction involving aqueous copper(II) sulfate and sodium hydroxide solution.

a Sodium hydroxide is an alkali. Define the term 'alkali'.

.... [1]

b Write a symbol equation, including state symbols, for the reaction between copper(II) sulfate and sodium hydroxide solution.

.... [2]

c Use the Periodic Table to calculate the mass of 1 mole of copper(II) hydroxide.

.... [1]

d In the reaction 50 cm^3 of 0.1M sodium hydroxide solution is used.

Calculate the number of moles of sodium hydroxide used.

....

.... [1]

e Sufficient copper(II) sulfate solution is used to react with all the sodium hydroxide solution. Use the equation to calculate the mass of copper(II) hydroxide produced in the reaction.

....

....

....

.... [3]

f In fact, after preparing the dry copper(II) hydroxide its mass was 0.2 g.

Calculate the percentage yield achieved in the experiment.

.... [2]

[Total: 10]

7 **a** In the boxes below sketch diagrams to represent a pure metal and an alloy.

Pure metal	Alloy

[2]

b Use your diagrams to explain why alloys can be stronger and harder than the pure metal they contain.

....

.... [2]

c The relative reactivity of metals can be determined by the results of displacement reactions. An example of a displacement reaction is shown below (X and W represent metals):

$$X(s) + W(NO_3)_2(aq) \rightarrow X(NO_3)_2(aq) + W(s)$$

i) Deduce the oxidation number of metal W in compound $W(NO_3)_2$.

.... [1]

ii) Deduce the charge on the metal ion X in the compound $X(NO_3)_2$.

.... [1]

iii) Which is the most reactive metal?

.... [1]

d Zinc is used in the process of galvanising to protect iron from corrosion. This is an example of sacrificial protection. Explain the meaning of sacrificial protection.

....

....

.... [2]

[Total: 9]

8 Ethanoic acid is a member of the homologous series of carboxylic acids.

a State the general formula of a carboxylic acid.

.... [1]

b Sketch the displayed formula of ethanoic acid.

[2]

c Ethanoic acid reacts with ethanol to form ethyl ethanoate and water.

i) Name the type of catalyst used in this reaction.

.... [1]

ii) What general name is given to compounds such as ethyl ethanoate?

.... [1]

iii) Sketch the displayed formula of ethyl ethanoate.

[2]

d The diagram represents part of the structure of nylon.

i) Deduce whether nylon is an addition polymer or a condensation polymer.

.... [1]

ii) One of the monomers has the functional group of $-NH_2$. What name is given to an organic compound with this functional group?

.... [1]

iii) What name is given to polymers like nylon which have monomers containing the $-COOH$ and $-NH_2$ functional groups?

.... [1]

iv) Proteins are natural polymers. Name the type of monomers that combine to form a protein.

.... [1]

v) Sketch a displayed formula of a typical monomer that combines to form a protein.

[2]
[Total: 13]

Periodic Table

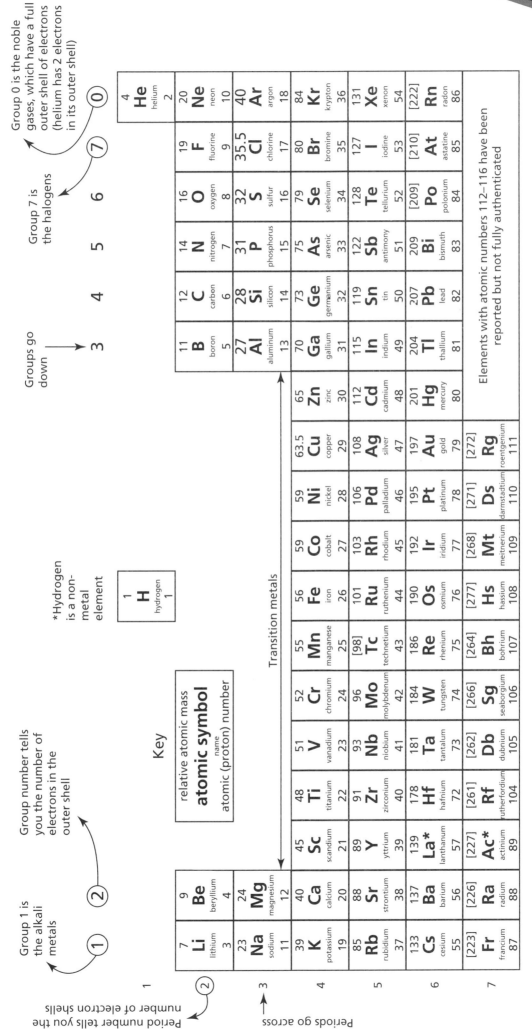

Group 1 is the alkali metals

Group number tells you the number of electrons in the outer shell

Group 0 is the noble gases, which have a full outer shell of electrons (helium has 2 electrons in its outer shell)

Group 7 is the halogens

Groups go down

Key

| relative atomic mass |
| **atomic symbol** |
| name |
| atomic (proton) number |

*Hydrogen is a non-metal element

| 1 |
| **H** |
| hydrogen |
| 1 |

Transition metals

Period number tells you the number of electron shells

Periods go across

* The Lanthanides (atomic numbers 58–71) and the Actinides (atomic numbers 90–103) have been omitted.
Relative atomic masses for **Cu** and **Cl** have not been rounded to the nearest whole number.

Elements with atomic numbers 112–116 have been reported but not fully authenticated

179

Instructions

- Answer **all** the questions.
- You may use a calculator.
- You should show your working and use appropriate units.
- Notes for use in qualitative analysis are provided in the question paper (pages 186–187).
- The total mark for this paper is 40. The time allowed is 1 hour.

1 You have been asked to prepare a pure sample of zinc chloride using the reaction between zinc carbonate and dilute hydrochloric acid.

a The stages of the preparation are listed below.

1. Excess zinc carbonate is added to 25 cm^3 of dilute hydrochloric acid in a beaker until all the acid has been reacted.
2. The zinc carbonate is removed and the remaining solution collected in a suitable container.
3. Dry crystals of zinc chloride are then obtained.

i) Explain how you would know that all the dilute hydrochloric acid had reacted in Stage 1.

.... [1]

ii) Describe the process that should be used in Stage 2 to remove the excess zinc carbonate.

.... [1]

iii) Give the general name for a solution collected as part of the process identified in part **(ii)**.

.... [1]

iv) Describe the process that should be used in Stage 3 to obtain the crystals of zinc chloride. You should include the names of any apparatus required.

....

....

....

.... [4]

b You are asked to carry out a test to confirm that the crystals are zinc chloride. Complete the table below with the tests you would conduct and the corresponding results for zinc chloride.

Ions formed when zinc chloride crystals dissolve in distilled water	Test used	Results confirming the identification	
Zinc ions	Add aqueous sodium hydroxide.		[1]
Chloride ions			[2]

[Total: 10]

2 ▶ The apparatus shown in the diagram is used to compare the thermal energy produced during the burning of three fuels, labelled X, Y and Z. The mass of the paraffin burner is measured before and after each experiment, along with the temperature rise of the water.

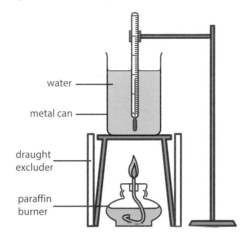

a Explain why a metal can is used instead of a glass beaker.

.... [1]

b Give **one** condition that should be the same for the burning of each fuel to ensure that the comparison of the three fuels is fair (a fair test).

.... [1]

c The results of the experiments are shown in the table. Complete the missing results.

Fuel	Rise in temperature of the water (°C)	Mass of spirit burner and fuel before burning (g)	Mass of spirit burner and fuel after burning (g)	Mass of fuel burnt (g)	Temperature rise per 1 g of fuel burnt (°C/g)
X	28	42.6	41.2		
Y	25	40.2	39.3		27.8
Z	27	44.3		1.5	

[2]

[1]

[2]

d Which fuel releases the most thermal energy per gram on burning?

.... [1]

[Total: 8]

3 The apparatus shown is used to investigate how the concentration of dilute nitric acid affects the rate of its reaction with magnesium ribbon.

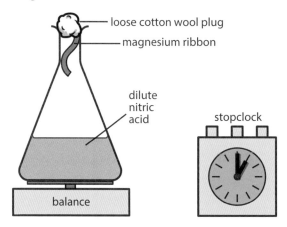

a Suggest a reason why magnesium ribbon is used instead of magnesium powder.

.... [1]

b The results of the first experiment using 1.0M nitric acid are shown in the table.

Time (s)	Mass of the conical flask (g)	Total loss in mass (g)
0	125.0	0.0
10	124.0	1.0
20	123.2	1.8
30	122.4	2.6
40	123.0	2.0
50	122.8	2.1
60	122.8	2.2
70	122.8	2.2
80	122.8	2.2

i) Which result appears to be anomalous?

.... [1]

ii) Plot on the graph paper the loss in mass (**g**) against the time (**seconds**) for the first experiment. Draw a smooth curve showing the pattern in the results.

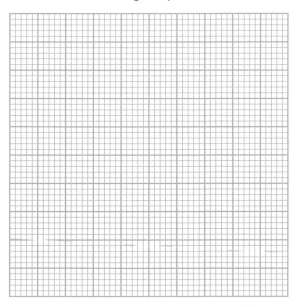

[3]

iii) The experiment is then repeated with 0.5M nitric acid. Give **one** condition that should not be changed when the second experiment is performed so that a comparison can be made with the first experiment.

.... [1]

iv) How will the rate of reaction in this second experiment compare with the rate of reaction in the first experiment?

.... [1]

v) On your graph draw a curve which shows the likely comparison with the curve obtained from the first experiment. Label this curve Experiment 2.   [2]

[**Total: 9**]

4 The apparatus shown below is used to collect the products formed from the electrolysis of dilute sulfuric acid.

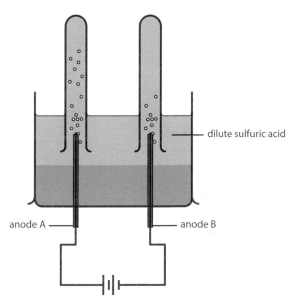

a Inert electrodes are used in the electrolysis. Suggest what the electrodes could be made of.

.... [1]

b The ions present in dilute sulfuric acid are H^+, OH^- and SO_4^{2-}.

i) Name the electrode labelled A.

.... [1]

ii) Identify the gas formed at electrode A.

.... [1]

iii) Describe a test and its result, which would confirm the presence of this gas at electrode A.

.... [1]

iv) Identify the gas formed at the electrode labelled B.

.... [1]

v) Describe a test and its result that would confirm the presence of this gas at electrode B.

.... [1]

[Total: 6]

5 Some tests were carried out to identify the names of two chemicals, P and Q. The table provides details of the tests and the results obtained. Use the information to identify chemicals P and Q.

Chemical	Test 1		Test 2		Chemical name
	Method	Result	Method	Result	
P	Add aqueous sodium hydroxide.	Green precipitate dissolves in excess sodium hydroxide solution giving a colourless solution.	Add sodium hydroxide solution and warm, add aluminium foil.	Gas produced which turned damp red litmus blue.	
Q	Flame test.	Yellow colour.	Add dilute nitric acid and silver nitrate solution.	Yellow precipitate formed	

[4]

6 Chromatography was used to identify the number of dyes in a sample of ink.

a Sketch and label a diagram showing how the experiment could be set up.

[2]

b The ink sample was shown to have one component. Sketch a chromatogram which shows the ink had only one component.

[1]
[Total: 3]

Notes for use in qualitative analysis

Tests for anions

Anion	Test	Test result
Carbonate, CO_3^{2-}	Add dilute acid, then test for carbon dioxide gas	Effervescence, carbon dioxide produced
Chloride, Cl^- [in solution]	Acidify with dilute nitric acid, then add aqueous silver nitrate	White ppt.
Bromide, Br^- [in solution]	Acidify with dilute nitric acid, then add aqueous silver nitrate	Cream ppt.
Iodide, I^- [in solution]	Acidify with dilute nitric acid, then add aqueous silver nitrate	Yellow ppt.
Nitrate, NO_3^- [in solution]	Add aqueous sodium hydroxide, then aluminium foil; warm carefully	Ammonia produced
Sulfate, SO_4^{2-} [in solution]	Acidify with dilute nitric acid, then add aqueous barium nitrate	White ppt.
Sulfite, SO_3^{2-}	Add a small volume of acidified aqueous potassium manganate(VII)	The acidified aqueous potassium manganate(VII) changes from purple to colourless

Tests for aqueous cations

Cation	Effect of aqueous sodium hydroxide	Effect of aqueous ammonia
Aluminium, Al^{3+}	White ppt., soluble in excess, giving a colourless solution	White ppt., insoluble in excess
Ammonium, NH_4^+	Ammonia produced on warming	–
Calcium, Ca^{2+}	White ppt., insoluble in excess	No ppt. or very slight white ppt.
Chromium(III), Cr^{3+}	Green ppt., soluble in excess	Green ppt., insoluble in excess
Copper(II), Cu^{2+}	Light blue ppt., insoluble in excess	Light blue ppt., soluble in excess, giving a Dark blue solution
Iron(II), Fe^{2+}	Green ppt., insoluble in excess, ppt. turns brown near surface on standing	Green ppt., insoluble in excess, ppt. turns Brown near surface on standing
Iron(III), Fe^{3+}	Red-brown ppt., insoluble in excess	Red-brown ppt., insoluble in excess
Zinc, Zn^{2+}	White ppt., soluble in excess, giving a colourless solution	White ppt., soluble in excess, giving a colourless solution

Tests for gases

Gas	Test and test result
Ammonia, NH_3	Turns damp red litmus paper blue
Carbon dioxide, CO_2	Turns limewater milky
Chlorine, Cl_2	Bleaches damp litmus paper
Hydrogen, H_2	'Pops' with a lighted splint
Oxygen, O_2	Relights a glowing splint
Sulfur dioxide, SO_2	Turns acidified aqueous potassium manganate(VII) from purple to colourless

Flame tests for metal ions

Metal ion	Flame colour
Lithium, Li^+	Red
Sodium, Na^+	Yellow
Potassium, K^+	Lilac
Calcium, Ca^{2+}	Orange-red
Barium, Ba^{2+}	Light green
Copper (II), Cu^{2+}	Blue-green

Pages 6–9: Section 1 Revise Questions

Page 7 Solids, liquids and gases Quick Test
1. A gas
2. Condensation
3. Increasing pressure, reducing temperature
4. **S** As the pressure is increased, the particles in the gas are forced closer together and the volume of the gas will decrease.
5. **S** Near room temperature

Page 9 Diffusion Quick Test
1. The mixing and moving of particles.
2. Liquids and gases
3. **S** 44
4. **S** Methane

Pages 10–21: Section 2 Revise Questions

Page 11 Atomic structure and the Periodic Table Quick Test
1. It is made up of a mixture of different gases, which are not chemically combined.
2. Zero
3. a) 12
   b)

$^{12}_{6}C$

   c) Carbon has four electrons in its outer electron shell, therefore it is in Group IV.
   d) The period number is 2 (carbon is in the 2nd period).

Page 13 Isotopes Quick Test
1. An atom of an element with the same number of protons but different numbers of neutrons to another atom of the same element.
2.

Symbol	Number of protons	Number of electrons	Number of neutrons
$^{39}_{19}K$	19	19	20

3. a) 8 protons, 8 neutrons
   b) 10 electrons arranged 2,8
4. **S** They have the same electron configuration/arrangement.
5. **S** The relative abundance of the two isotopes.

Page 15 Ions and ionic bonds Quick Test
1. A positive ion
2. a) One
   b) 1 + (K^+)
3. High melting point. Calcium chloride is an ionic compound with strong forces of electrostatic attraction between the oppositely charged ions.
4. **S** Aluminium loses three electrons forming Al^{3+}, oxygen gains two electrons to form O^{2-}; so two Al atoms lose six electrons, and three O atoms gain those six electrons.
5. **S** A giant ionic lattice is a regular arrangement of positive and negative ions.

Page 17 Simple molecules and covalent bonds Quick Test
1. The sharing of a pair of electrons leading to noble gas configurations.

2. a) 7 electrons (it is in Group VII of the Periodic Table)
   b) 2 electrons
   c)

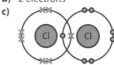

3. Hydrogen will not conduct electricity.
4. **S** In ethene there are weak intermolecular forces.

Page 19 Giant covalent structures Quick Test
1. a) 4; b) 3
2. The delocalised electrons between the layers.
3. **S** 4
4. **S** In a giant structure all the atoms are strongly bonded; in a simple molecular structure there are weak forces between the molecules.

Page 21 Metallic bonding Quick Test
1. **S** A positive ion
2. **S** The electrons are delocalised and so can move freely.
3. **S** Copper is a good electrical conductor and is ductile so can be drawn into wires.
4. **S** Can be beaten into sheets.
5. **S** Diamond/graphite/silicon(IV) oxide

Pages 22–27: Section 3 Revise Questions

Page 23 Formulae Quick Test
1. $MgCl_2$
2. $4Na(s) + O_2(g) \rightarrow 2Na_2O(s)$
3. **S** $Fe^{3+}(aq) + 3OH^-(aq) \rightarrow Fe(OH)_3(s)$

Page 25 Relative masses of atoms and molecules Quick Test
1. The average mass of the isotopes of an element compared to 1/12th of the mass of an atom of ^{12}C.
2. 180
3. 138
4. 132 g

Page 26 The mole and the Avogadro constant Quick Test
1. **S** Room temperature and pressure
2. **S** 0.5 moles
3. **S** 0.25 moles
4. **S** 1.204×10^{24}
5. **S** 1.5 dm³

Pages 28–41: Sections 1–3 Practise Questions

Page 28 Solids, liquids and gases
1. B [1]
2. B [1]
3. a) Increasing temperature will increase the volume of a gas. [1]
   b) Reducing pressure will increase the volume of the gas. [1]
4. **S** The sketch shows:
   - the axes labelled as Temperature (°C) and Time (minutes) [1]
   - starting temperature at 20°C finishing temperature 100°C [1]
   - gradient of curve decreasing as the temperature rises and levelling off at 100°C [1]
5. **S** a) The particles in the liquid gain energy and move more rapidly. [1] The forces of attraction between some particles are broken. [1]

   b) The gas particles are able to move further apart. [1]
      The volume of the gas will decrease. [1]

Page 28 Diffusion
1. As the particles in the crystal start to dissolve, the forces between the particles decrease [1]; and the particles start to move further away from each other. [1]
2. a) Do the experiment in a fume cupboard / do not inhale the bromine gas. [1] Remove the gas jar lids very carefully to prevent bromine gas escaping. [1]
   b) The gas particles of air and bromine have enough energy to move constantly. [1] The particles of the two gases will mix. [1]
   c) Bromine particles/molecules have a greater mass than the particles of the gases in air [1]; and so will not move as far apart. [1]
3. a) i) 2 [1]
      S ii) 32 [1]
      iii) 44 [1]
      iv) 71 [1]
   b) Hydrogen will diffuse the most rapidly [1]; as it has the smallest relative molecular mass. [1]
   c) Chlorine will diffuse the least rapidly [1]; as it has the highest relative molecular mass. [1]

Page 30 Atomic structure and the Periodic Table
1. C [1]
2. B [1]
3. B [1]
4. a) 8 electrons [1]
   b) 2,6 [1]
   c) Group 6 [1]; it has six electrons in its outer electron shell. [1]
   d)

   Correct nucleus arrangement [1]; correct electron configuration [1]
5. a) The potassium atom: 19 protons, 19 electrons, 20 neutrons [1]
   b) The potassium ion: 19 protons, 18 electrons, 20 neutrons [1]

Page 31 Isotopes
1. D [1]
2. C [1]
3. a)

Isotopes	Number of protons	Number of neutrons	Number of electrons	Relative Abundance (%)
$^{69}_{31}Ga$	31	38	31	60
$^{71}_{31}Ga$	31	40	31	40

   b) The two gallium atoms have the same number of electrons [1]; and the same electronic configuration. [1]
   c) There are three electrons in the outer electron shell. [1]

d) The relative atomic mass of gallium

$$= \frac{(69 \times 60) + (71 \times 40)}{100} \ [1]$$

$$= \frac{4140 + 2840}{100} \ [1]$$

$$= 69.8 \ [1]$$

Page 32 Ions and ionic bonds

1. C [1]
2. B [1]
3. C [1]
4. a)

Element	Atomic number	Electron arrangement
Sodium	11	2,8,1 [1]
Fluorine	9	2,7 [1]

b) Formula = NaF [1]

c)

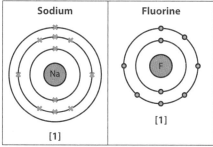

[1]

d)

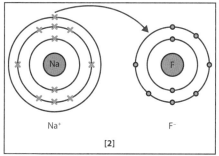

[2]

5. **S**

a)

Element	Atomic Number	Electron arrangement
Aluminium	13 [1]	2,8,3 [1]
Oxygen	8 [1]	2,6 [1]

b)

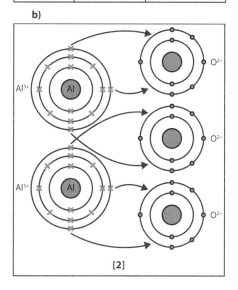

[2]

c)

Property	Prediction/explanation
Melting point	High. Strong forces between the ions in the solid state. [2]
Boiling point	High. Strong forces between the ions in the liquid state. [2]
Electrical conductivity	Good. The ions are free to move to the electrodes and produce a flow of electrons. [2]

6. **S** Each ion surrounded by six ions of the opposite charge [1]; in a 3D arrangement with strong forces between the ions. [1]

Page 34 Simple molecules and covalent bonds

1. D [1]
2. D [1]
3. a)

Element	Electron arrangement
Hydrogen	1 [1]
Chlorine	2,8,7 [1]

b) Formula = HCl [1]

c) Hydrogen

hydrogen

Chlorine [2]

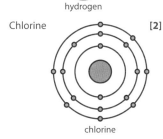

chlorine

d) [2]

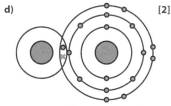

4. **a)** **S** [2]

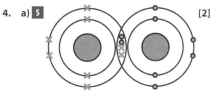

b)

Property	Prediction/explanation
Melting point	Low. Weak intermolecular forces [2]
Boiling point	Low. Weak intermolecular forces [2]
Electrical conductivity	Poor. No ions or electrons free to move. [2]

5. **S** [3]

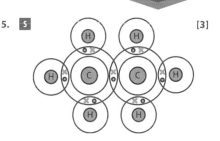

Page 36 Giant covalent structures

1. D [1]
2. a)

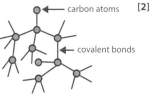

carbon atoms [2]

covalent bonds

b) In diamond, each carbon atom is covalently bonded to four other carbon atoms. [1] In graphite, each carbon atom is covalently bonded to three other carbon atoms. [1]

3. **a)** **S** Both will have high melting/boiling points [1]; as both the carbon and silicon atoms are strongly covalently bonded to four other atoms. [1]

b) Both will have high melting/boiling points. [1] Unlike sodium chloride, silicon(IV) oxide will not act as an electrolyte [1]; as it does not contain any ions. [1]

Page 37 Metallic bonding

1. **S** **a)** The metal structure involves positive ions surrounded by delocalised electrons. [1] The electrons can move when a current is applied to the solid. [1]

b) There is a strong electrostatic attraction [1]; between the ions and the delocalised electrons. [1]

c) The metal ions can move within the delocalised electron cloud [1]; so can be drawn into wires. [1]

2. **S** **a)** A [1]
b) D [1]
c) B [1]
d) C [1]

3. **S** **a)**

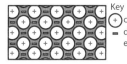

Key
+ cation
– delocalised electron

[2]

b) The metal structure involves positive ions surrounded by delocalised electrons. [1] The electrons can move when a current is applied to the solid. [1]

c) The metal ions can move within the delocalised electron cloud [1]; so the metal can be beaten into sheets. [1]

Page 38 Formulae

1. B [1]
2. C [1]
3. **a)** magnesium(s) + oxygen(g) → magnesium oxide(s) [1]
b) $2Mg(s) + O_2(g) \rightarrow 2MgO(s)$ [2]
4. **S** B [1]
5. **S** AlF_3 [1]

6. a) $\boxed{S}$ $Ca(s) + 2H_2O(l) \rightarrow$
        $Ca(OH)_2(aq) + H_2(g)$ [2]
    b) $Ca(s) + 2H_2O(l) \rightarrow Ca^{2+}(aq)$
        $+ 2OH^-(aq) + H_2(g)$ [2]
7. $\boxed{S}$ $Mg(s) + Cu^{2+}(aq) \rightarrow$
    $Mg^{2+}(aq) + Cu(s)$ [2]

Page 39 Relative masses of atoms and molecules

1. a) The ^{12}C atom [1]
    b) There are isotopes of chlorine – 35.5 is the average mass. [1]
2. a) 40 [1]
    b) 102 [1]
    c) 46 [1]
    d) 60 [1]
3. a) 16 g [2]
    b) 18 g [2]
4. a) $C_3H_8 + 5O_2 \rightarrow 3CO_2 + 4H_2O$ [2]
    b) 66 g [2]
5. a) $Fe_2O_3 + 3CO \rightarrow 2Fe + 3CO_2$ [2]
    b) i) 700 g [3]
       ii) 825 g [3]

Page 40 The mole and the Avogadro constant

1. Moles per cubic decimetre/litre (also accept concentration) [1]
2. $\boxed{S}$ C [1]
3. $\boxed{S}$ D [1]
4. $\boxed{S}$

Number of particles	Mass of water (H$_2$O)
6.02×10^{23}	1 mole = 18 g [1]
6.02×10^{22}	1.8 g [1]
3.01×10^{22}	0.9 g [1]

5. $\boxed{S}$ $\frac{39}{39} = 1$ and $\frac{8}{16} = 0.5$ [1]
    Therefore, ratio = 2 : 1, so K_2O [1]
6. $\boxed{S}$ a) $2Ca + O_2 \rightarrow 2CaO$ [2]
    b) moles of CaO $= \frac{7}{56} = 0.125$ [1]
       moles of Ca $= 0.125 \times 40 = 5$ g [1]
    c) $\frac{5}{7} = 0.714$ [2]
       $0.71 \times 100 = 71.4\%$
7. $\boxed{S}$ a)

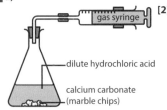

[2]

gas syringe
dilute hydrochloric acid
calcium carbonate (marble chips)

    b) $CaCO_3(s) + 2HCl(aq) \rightarrow$
       $CaCl_2(aq) + CO_2(g) + H_2O(l)$ [2]
    c) 100 g and 24 dm^3 [1]
       0.2 g: $24 \times \frac{0.2}{100} = 0.048$ dm^3 [2]
8. $\boxed{S}$ a)

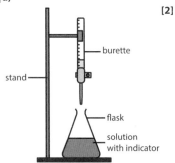

[2]

burette
stand
flask
solution with indicator

---

b) $HCl + NaOH \rightarrow NaCl + H_2O$ [2]
c) i) To obtain an accurate result/average result. [1]
   ii)

HCl	NaOH	
1 mole	1 mole	[1]
1000 cm^3 0.1M	1000 cm^3 0.1M	[1]
20 cm^3 0.1M	25 cm^3	

   $0.1 \times \frac{25}{20} = 0.125M$ [1]

Pages 42-43: Section 4 Revise Questions

Page 43 Electrolysis and hydrogen-oxygen fuel cells Quick Test

1. The ions in the electrolyte must be able to move.
2. a) $\boxed{S}$ Hydrogen is less reactive than potassium.
    b) $\boxed{S}$ $2H^+(aq) + 2e- \rightarrow H_2(g)$

Pages 44-45: Section 5 Revise Questions

Page 45 Exothermic and endothermic reactions Quick Test

1. An endothermic reaction takes in thermal energy from the surroundings, leading to a decrease in the temperature of the surroundings.
2. $\boxed{S}$ Activation energy is the minimum energy that colliding particles must have to react.

Pages 46-51: Section 6 Revise Questions

Page 47 Physical and chemical changes, rate of reaction Quick Test

1. Increasing temperature will increase the rate of reaction.
2. a) The rate of a reaction should decrease as the reaction proceeds.
    b) $\boxed{S}$ The number of collisions between the reacting particles decreases as the particles react together.
3. a) It will increase.
    b) $\boxed{S}$ The number of reacting particles increases / there will be more collisions between the magnesium and hydrochloric acid particles.
    c) Sources of error: the mass is not measured accurately every 10 seconds; there are inaccuracies in timing.

Page 49 Reversible reactions and equilibrium Quick Test

1. Increasing temperature will favour the formation of anhydrous copper(II) sulfate. Adding water will favour the formation of hydrated copper(II) sulfate.
2. $\boxed{S}$ a) Increases the amount of W.
    b) Reduces the amount of W.
    c) No effect on the equilibrium.
3. $\boxed{S}$ a) Air
    b) Methane

Page 51 Redox Quick Test

1. Reduction is the loss of oxygen.
2. a) Aluminium has been oxidised.
    b) Copper(II) oxide has been reduced.
3. $\boxed{S}$ Oxidation is the loss of electrons.
4. $\boxed{S}$ a) Mg has an oxidation number of zero.
    b) Magnesium has been oxidised.
    c) Magnesium is the reducing agent.

Pages 52-55: Section 7 Revise Questions

Page 53 The characteristic properties of acids and bases Quick Test

1. Blue
2. a) A base
    b) $ZnO(s) +$
       $2HCl(aq) \rightarrow ZnCl_2(aq) + H_2O(l)$
    c) $\boxed{S}$ A proton donor
3. a) $\boxed{S}$ Hydrochloric acid is a strong acid; ethanoic acid is a weak acid.
    b) The pH of hydrochloric acid, a strong acid, will be lower than the pH of ethanoic acid, a weak acid.

Page 55 Oxides and preparation of salts Quick Test

1. Basic
2. $\boxed{S}$ A basic oxide reacts with an acid to form a salt. An amphoteric oxide reacts with both an acid and an alkali to form a salt.
3. Solution heated until crystals start to form, then left to cool so water evaporates.
4. $\boxed{S}$ Precipitate
5. $\boxed{S}$ Water of crystallisation

Pages 56-65: Sections 4-7 Practise Questions

Page 56 Electrolysis and hydrogen–oxygen fuel cells

1. a) Anode connected to the positive terminal of the battery. [1]
    b) Cathode connected to the negative terminal of the battery. [1]
2. a)

Electrolyte	Product at the anode	Product at the cathode
Molten lead(II) bromide	bromine [1]	lead [1]
Dilute sulfuric acid	oxygen [1]	hydrogen [1]

    b) Carbon/graphite/platinum [1]
3. To improve resistance to corrosion. [1]
4. D [1]
5. $\boxed{S}$ a) Aluminium [1]
    b) $Al^{3+} + 3e^- \rightarrow Al$ [2]
6. $\boxed{S}$ a)

Electrolyte	Product at the anode	Product at the cathode
Dilute aqueous sodium iodide	Hydrogen [1]	Oxygen [1]
Concentrated aqueous sodium iodide	Hydrogen [1]	Iodine [1]

    b) $2I^- \rightarrow I_2 + 2e^-$ [2]
7. $\boxed{S}$ a) Copper anode dissolving and losing mass. [1]
    b) Copper being deposited and cathode gaining mass. [1]

Page 57 Exothermic and endothermic reactions

1. a) An exothermic reaction transfers thermal energy to the surroundings [1]; causing an increase in temperature of the surroundings. [1]
    b) i) $Mg + 2HCl \rightarrow MgCl_2 + H_2$ [2]
       ii) An insulated cup [1]; to prevent transfer of thermal energy to and from the surroundings. [1]
       iii) A 30°C/g [1]
            B 25°C/g [1]
            C 30°C/g [1]
       iv) Group B [1]

2. [S]
a)

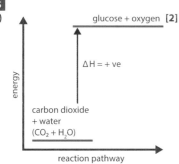

glucose + oxygen **[2]**

$\Delta H = +$ ve

carbon dioxide + water $(CO_2 + H_2O)$

energy

reaction pathway

b) Activation energy is the minimum energy that colliding particles must have for a reaction to take place. **[1]**

3. [S] $C_3H_8(g) + 5O_2(g) \rightarrow 3CO_2(g) + 4H_2O(l)$ **[2]**
$(8 \times 416) + (2 \times 356) + (5 \times 498) = +6530$
$(6 \times 803) + (4 \times 467) = +8544$ **[2]**
$\Delta H_r = +6530 - +8554 = -2024$ kJ/mol **[2]**

Page 59 Physical and chemical changes, rate of reaction

1. D **[1]**
2. C **[1]**
3. a)

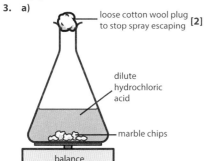

loose cotton wool plug to stop spray escaping **[2]**

dilute hydrochloric acid

marble chips

balance

b) 3 headings **[1]**; 1 minute in 10 s readings. **[1]**

Time (s)	Mass (g)	Loss in mass (g)
0		
10		
20		
30		
40		
50		
60		

c) **[2]**

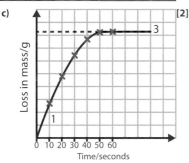

Loss in mass/g

Time/seconds

4. [S] a) Increasing temperature: greater kinetic energy of particles **[1]**; more successful collisions. **[1]**
b) Increasing concentration: more particles in a particular volume **[1]**; more effective collisions. **[1]**

c) Using powder rather than ribbon: greater surface area / more particles near the surface **[1]**; more effective collisions. **[1]**

5. [S] a) Experiment 1 **[1]**
b) The steeper gradient **[1]** indicates a faster rate of reaction. **[1]**
c) One of the reactants is used up / the reaction is complete **[1]**; there are no further collisions. **[1]**

6. [S] a)

activation energy (E_a)

Energy

reactants

enthalpy change, ΔH

products

Reaction pathway

Correctly labelled: reactant and product **[1]**, enthalpy change **[1]**, activation energy **[1]**

b) Activation energy is the minimum energy needed for a reaction **[1]**; from the collisions of reacting particles. **[1]**
c) A catalyst lowers the activation energy. **[1]**

Page 60 Reversible reactions and equilibrium

1. C **[1]**
2. [S] a) Rate of the forward reaction = rate of the reverse reaction **[1]**
b) The concentrations of reactants and products do not change. **[1]**
3. [S] a) $N_2(g) + 3H_2(g) \rightleftharpoons 2NH_3(g)$ **[2]**
b) i) Air **[1]**
   ii) Methane **[1]**
c)

Conditions	High	Low
Temperature		✓ **[1]**
Pressure	✓ **[1]**	

d) i) Iron **[1]**
   ii) The catalyst has no effect on the equilibrium position. **[1]**
4. [S] a) $2SO_2(g) + O_2(g) \rightleftharpoons 2SO_3(g)$ **[2]**
b) i) 450°C (allow 400–500°C) **[1]**
   ii) 200 kPa / 2 atm (allow 150–250 kPa) **[1]**
   iii) Vanadium(V) oxide **[1]**
5. [S] The high temperature provides a better rate of reaction **[1]**; even though the conversion to products is less. **[1]**

Page 62 Redox

1. C **[1]**
2. A reaction that involves simultaneous oxidation and reduction. **[1]**
3. a) Mg **[1]**; b) CuO **[1]**
4. [S] a) Ca **[1]**
b) $0 \rightarrow +2$ **[1]**
c) Cl_2 **[1]**
d) $0 \rightarrow -1$ **[1]**
5. [S] a) Ag^+ **[1]**
b) Mg **[1]**
6. [S] a) Purple to colourless **[1]**
b) $+7 \rightarrow +2$ **[1]**
c) Reduced **[1]**

Page 63 The characteristic properties of acids and bases

1. C **[1]**
2. C **[1]**
3. a) Potassium chloride **[1]**
b) Neutralisation **[1]**
c) $HCl(aq) + KOH(aq) \rightarrow KCl(aq) + H_2O(l)$ **[2]**
d) $H^+(aq) + OH^-(aq) \rightarrow H_2O(l)$ **[2]**
4. [S] B **[1]**
5. [S] a) Proton donor **[1]**
b) Hydrochloric acid **[1]**
c) A strong acid is completely dissociated in aqueous solution. **[1]**
d) $HCl(aq) \rightarrow H^+(aq) + Cl^-(aq)$ **[2]**

Page 66 Oxides and preparation of salts

1. C **[1]**
2. A **[1]**
3. D **[1]**
4. a) A substance that is chemically combined with water. **[1]**
b) Anhydrous **[1]**
5. a) $Mg(s) + H_2SO_4(aq) \rightarrow MgSO_4(aq) + H_2(g)$ **[2]**
b)

Preparation	Magnesium ribbon/powder added to the dilute sulfuric acid. **[1]**
	Until no further reaction. **[1]**
Separation	Filter to remove excess magnesium. **[1]**
	Collect the filtrate in an evaporating basin. **[1]**
Purification	Heat the solution in the evaporating dish until ready to crystallise. **[1]**
	Leave to cool and crystallise. **[1]**

6. a) Carbon dioxide **[1]**
b) $MgCO_3(s) + H_2SO_4(aq) \rightarrow MgSO_4(aq) + CO_2(g) + H_2O(l)$ **[2]**
7. a) Hydrochloric acid **[1]**
b) Burette **[1]**
c) Sodium hydroxide **[1]**
d) Pipette **[1]**
e)

Name of indicator	Colour in alkali	Colour in acid
Methyl orange	Yellow	Red
or		
thymolphthalein **[1]**	Blue **[1]**	Colourless **[1]**

8. [S] a) A solid formed in a solution / when solutions are mixed. **[1]**
b) $Pb(NO_3)_2(aq) + 2HCl(aq) \rightarrow PbCl_2(s) + 2HNO_3(aq)$ **[2]**
c)

Preparation	Mix the two solutions. **[1]**
Separation	Filter the mixture. **[1]**
Purification	Wash the precipitate with water. **[1]**
	Leave to dry. **[1]**

9. [S] a) Water of crystallisation **[1]**
b) The water is chemically bonded to the cobalt(II) chloride. **[1]**

Pages 66-73: Section 8 Revise Questions

Page 67 Arrangement of elements Quick Test
1. A row in the Periodic Table.
2. Element in Group V.
3. a) 2,8,6; b) 2^-

ANSWERS

4. **S** The trend is an increase in boiling point down the group.

Page 69 Group I properties Quick Test
1. The melting point of caesium will be lower than that of potassium.
2. Rubidium will be more reactive than sodium.
3. $4Li(s) + O_2(g) \rightarrow 2Li_2O(s)$
4. $2K(s) + 2H_2O(l) \rightarrow 2KOH(aq) + H_2(g)$

Page 71 Group VII properties Quick Test
1. A grey-black solid
2. The density of bromine will be greater than the density of chlorine.
3. Fluorine
4. $Cl_2(g) + 2NaI(aq) \rightarrow 2NaCl(aq) + I_2(aq)$

Page 73 Transition elements and noble gases Quick Test
1. The melting point of copper will be much higher than that for sodium.
2. A substance that changes/ increases the rate of a chemical reaction but is unchanged at the end of the reaction.
3. **S** +7 (+VII)
4. The noble gases have full outer electron shells.
5. The term monatomic means that the elements exist as single atoms.

Pages 74-81: Section 9 Revise Questions

Page 75 Properties of metals Quick Test
1. Ductile; good electrical conductivity
2. **a)** potassium + water → potassium hydoxide + hydrogen
   b) $2K(s) + 2H_2O(l) \rightarrow 2KOH(aq) + H_2(g)$
3. $Zn(s) + 2HCl(aq) \rightarrow ZnCl_2(aq) + H_2(g)$

Page 77 Uses of metals, alloys and their properties Quick Test
1. Iron has a higher density than aluminium and corrodes in the present of air and water. (The iron(III) oxide formed flakes off the metal, leaving it free to be oxidised further.)
2. The ductility of a metal is a measure of how readily it can be drawn into a wire.
3. An alloy is a mixture of a metal with other elements.
4. Brass contains copper and zinc.
5. **S** The added element breaks up the regular structure of the metal and stops the rows of atoms from sliding over each other.

Page 79 Reactivity series Quick Test
1. Potassium.
2. **a)** Zinc will not displace calcium.
   b) Calcium is more reactive than zinc.
3. **S** A layer of aluminium oxide covers the surface of the aluminium.
4. **S** $Zn(s) + 2AgNO_3(aq) \rightarrow$ $Zn(NO_3)_2(aq) + 2Ag(s)$

Page 81 Corrosion of metals and extraction Quick Test
1. The presence of air/oxygen and water.
2. **S** Even when the barrier is broken, oxygen and water will react with the zinc rather than the iron.
3. Haematite / iron(III) oxide, carbon / coke, limestone / calcium carbonate.
4. Carbon monoxide
5. **S** The cryolite lowers the melting point of the electrolyte (so saves money).

Pages 82-91: Sections 8-9 Practise Questions

Page 82 Arrangement of elements
1. C [1]
2. C [1]
3. A [1]
4. **a)** i) y [1]
   ii) [1]
   b) y [1]
   c) i) q [1]
   ii) The electron configuration of chlorine shows it is in Group VII. [1] All elements in Group VII will have seven electrons in the outer electron shell. [1]
5. **S** Melting point – no overall trend (magnesium lowest). [1]
   Boiling point – no overall trend (magnesium lowest). [1]
   Density decreases down the three elements (group). [1]

Page 83 Group I properties
1. D [1]
2. **a)** i) More rapid [1]
   ii) Reactivity increases down the group. [1]
   b) Alkaline [1]
   c) pH 8–14 [1]
   d) Effervescence/ bubbling as gas given off [1]; sodium dissolves [1]
   e) $2Na(s) + 2H_2O(l) \rightarrow 2NaOH(aq) + H_2(g)$ [2]
3. **a)** i) Rb^+ [1]
   ii) It has one electron in its outer electron shell / all Group I elements form single positive ions. [1]
   b) i) Stored under oil [1]
   ii) Basic oxide [1]; rubidium is a metal and the oxides of metals are basic. [1]
   iii) $4Rb(s) + O_2(g) \rightarrow 2Rb_2O(s)$ [2]
   c) $Rb_2O(s) + H_2O(l) \rightarrow 2RbOH(aq)$ [2]

Page 84 Group VII properties
1. D [1]
2. B [1]
3. **a)** A red-brown liquid [1]
   b) The density of bromine is less than the density of iodine. [1]
   c) Bromine is less reactive than fluorine. [1]
   d) Bromine has seven electrons in its outer electron shell. [1] Gaining one electron will create a full electron shell. [1]
   e) i) A more reactive element displaces a less reactive element from a solution of its salt. [1]
   ii) Potassium bromide [1]; and iodine [1]
   iii) Colourless potassium iodide [1]; will turn brown [1]
   iv) $Br_2(aq) + 2KI(aq) \rightarrow 2KBr(aq) + I_2(aq)$ [2]
4. $Cl_2(g) + 2I^-(aq) \rightarrow 2Cl^-(aq) + I_2(aq)$ [2]

Page 85 Transition elements and noble gases
1. A [1]
2. **a)** These are the oxidation numbers of copper in the compounds. [1]

b)

Name of the compound	Metal ion present	Formula of the compound
Copper(I) oxide	Cu^+ [1]	Cu_2O [1]
Copper(II) sulfate	Cu^{2+} [1]	$CuSO_4$ [1]

3. Haber process / manufacture of ammonia [1]
4. $CuO(s) + H_2SO_4(aq) \rightarrow CuSO_4(aq) + H_2O(l)$ [2]
5. **a)** 18 [1]
   b) 22 [1]
   c) 2,8,8 [1]
   d) It has a full outer electron shell. [1]
   e) It exists as a single atom. [1]

Page 86 Properties of metals
1. C [1]
2. Malleable means easily beaten into sheets. [1]
3. B [1]
4. **a)** sodium + oxygen → sodium oxide [1]
   b) $4Na(s) + O_2(g) \rightarrow 2Na_2O(s)$ [2]
5. **a)** Hydrogen [1]
   b) $Zn(s) + H_2SO_4(aq) \rightarrow ZnSO_4(aq) + H_2(g)$ [2]
6. **a)** A lilac / light purple flame [1]; effervescence / cube moving on surface of water / cube dissolving [1]
   b) Potassium hydroxide [1]; hydrogen [1]
   c) Litmus paper turns blue [1]
   d) $2K(s) + 2H_2O(l) \rightarrow 2KOH(aq) + H_2(g)$ [2]
7. $Mg(s) + H_2O(g) \rightarrow MgO(s) + H_2(g)$ [2]

Page 87 Uses of metals, alloys and their properties
1. Low density [1]; good electrical conductivity [1]
2. Good electrical conductivity [1]; ductility [1]
3. Iron corrodes/reacts with oxygen and water [1]; the iron(III) oxide flakes off / leaving the iron to corrode more. [1]
4. Shiny appearance [1]; does not corrode / react with oxygen and water [1]
5. C [1]
6. **a)** Iron [1]
   b) Hardness [1]; resistance to corrosion [1]
7. **a)** [1]

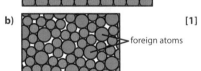

   b) [1] ← foreign atoms
8. **S** In an alloy the added element breaks up the regular structure [1]; the layers of atoms cannot slide over each other. [1]

Page 87 Reactivity series
1. C [1]
2. C [1]
3. **a)** Q Z W [1]

b)

Metals	Possible name
Q	Potassium, sodium or calcium [1]
W	Silver or gold [1]
Z	Magnesium, zinc or iron [1]

4. a) magnesium + sulfuric acid →
magnesium sulfate + hydrogen [1]
b) $Mg(s) + H_2SO_4(g) \rightarrow MgSO_4(s) + H_2(g)$ [2]
5. a) zinc + hydrochloric acid → zinc chloride + hydrogen [1]
b) $Zn(s) + 2HCl(aq) \rightarrow ZnCl_2(aq) + H_2(g)$ [2]
6. a) Reduction is the loss of oxygen. [1]
b) $2Fe_2O_3(s) + 3C(s) \rightarrow 4Fe(s) + 3CO_2(g)$ [2]
7. a) **S** Calcium has a greater tendency to form ions than zinc does. [1]
b) Ca^{2+} [1]
8. **S** a) Displacement reaction [1]
b) Zinc is more reactive than silver. [1]
c) $Zn + 2Ag^+ \rightarrow Zn^{2+} + 2Ag$ [2]
d) Any metal more reactive than silver (for example magnesium, iron or copper) [1]
9. **S** Aluminium is reactive and combines with oxygen [1]; aluminium oxide forms a barrier around the aluminium, preventing further reaction. [1]

Page 89 Corrosion of metals and extraction of metals
1. Hydrated iron(III) oxide [1]
2. a) Greasing/coating with plastic (allow galvanising) [1]
b) Excluding oxygen [1]; and water [1]
c) The paint my become scratched / peel off the iron. [1]
3. **S** a) Zinc [1]
b) Zinc is a more reactive metal than iron [1]; and so will react in preference to iron. [1]
4. a) Gold/silver [1]
b) Fe_2O_3 [1]
5. a) Carbon dioxide [1]
b) Reduction (allow redox) [1]
c) Reduction (allow redox) [1]
d) The limestone combines with sand and forms slag. [1]
6. C [1]
7. **S** a) $Fe_2O_3(s) + 3CO(g) \rightarrow 2Fe(s) + 3CO_2(g)$ [2]
b) $CaCO_3 \rightarrow CaO + CO_2$ [2]
c) $CaO + SiO_2 \rightarrow CaSiO_3$ [2]
8. **S** a) To lower the melting point. [1]
b) Carbon [1]
c) Cathode [1]
d) $Al^{3+} + 3e^- \rightarrow Al$ [2]
$2O^{2-} \rightarrow O_2 + 4e^-$ [2]

Pages 92-95: Section 10 Revise Questions

Page 93 Water and fertilisers Quick Test
1. a) Anhydrous means without water.
b) Colour change from blue to pink.
2. Fertilisers are the major source.
3. a) NH_4NO_3
b) Ammonium hydroxide and nitric acid

Page 95 Air quality and climate Quick Test
1. Less than 1%
2. Carbon monoxide
3. Methane

4. **S** The methane absorbs and reflects thermal energy preventing it escaping from the surface of the Earth. This thermal energy increases the global temperature of Earth's atmosphere.

Pages 96-108: Section 11 Revise Questions

Page 97 Fuels Quick Test
1. Methane
2. A compound that contains hydrogen and carbon only.
3. Short chain length
4. Bitumen is used in the building and maintenance of road surfaces.

Page 99 Alkanes Quick Test
1. A homologous series is a family of similar compounds with similar chemical properties.
2. C_nH_2n+2
3. $C_3H_8 + 5O_2 \rightarrow 3CO_2 + 4H_2O$
4. **S** a) In a substitution reaction one atom or group of atoms is replaced by another atom or group of atoms.
b) $C_3H_8 + Cl_2 \rightarrow C_3H_7Cl + HCl$

Page 101 Alkenes Quick Test
1. C_nH_{2n}
2. An unsaturated hydrocarbon has one or more carbon–carbon bonds that are not single bonds.
3. Add bromine or aqueous bromine. The bromine will be decolourised by an alkene.
4. **S** a) Nickel catalyst
b) $C_3H_6 + H_2 \rightarrow C_3H_8$

Page 103 Alcohols Quick Test
1. $C_nH_{2n}OH$
2. Temperature 300°C, pressure 6000 kPa / 60 atm.
3. Butanol will have the highest boiling point.
4. **S** It is a slow process.

Page 105 Carboxylic acids Quick Test
1. $C_nH_{2n+1}COOH$
2. A weak acid is only partially dissociated into ions.
3. a) $CuO + 2CH_3COOH \rightarrow Cu(CH_3COO)_2 + H_2O$
b) Copper(II) ethanoate
c) A salt
4. **S** An acid catalyst

Page 107 Polymers Quick Test
1. A polymer is a large molecule formed from smaller molecules called monomers.
2. Disposal in land fill sites; accumulation in oceans; formation of toxic gases when burnt.
3. **S** An addition polymer is made from one type of monomer. A condensation polymer is made from two different monomers.
4. **S** It can be recycled by converting it back to the monomers and re-polymerised.

Pages 108-115: Sections 10-11 Practise Questions

Page 108 Water and fertilisers
1. D [1]
2. A [1]
3. A [1]
4. a) Find the melting point of ice formed from the sample or find the boiling point of the sample. [1]

b) If sample is pure the melting point would be 0°C / if pure, the boiling point would be 100 °C at standard atmospheric pressure [1]
5.

	Stages	What the stage achieves
1.	Sedimentation/ filtration [1]	Removes solids
2.	Use of carbon	Removes tastes and odours [1]
3.	Chlorination [1]	Kills microbes

6. a) Phosphates remove oxygen from the water (deoxygenate). [1]
b) Nitrogen [1]; potassium [1]

Page 108 Air quality and climate
1. C [1]
2. C [1]
3. a) Photosynthesis [1]
b) carbon dioxide + water → glucose + oxygen [2]
c) Chlorophyll [1]
4. a) Carbon dioxide [1]; methane [1]
b)

Actions being taken to reduce climate change	What the actions achieve
1. Replacing fossil fuels by using solar and wind as sources of energy.	Reduces the amount of carbon dioxide produced. [1]
2. Improving the digestion in animals. [1]	Reduces the amount of methane produced. [1]
3. Planting trees. [1]	Reduces the amount of carbon dioxide by increasing photosynthesis. [1]

5. a) Sulfur dioxide [1]
b) From the combustion of fossil fuels [1]; containing sulfur. [1]
c) Using low-sulfur fuels [1]; using flue gas desulfurisation. [1]
6. **S** B [1]
7. **S** The absorption (of thermal energy) by the atmosphere. [1]
The reflection (of thermal energy) back to the surface of the Earth. [1]
The emission (of thermal energy) by the heated gases/surface. [1]
8. **S** a) Nitrogen gas reacts with oxygen gas (at high temperatures). [1]
b) $N_2(g) + O_2(g) \rightarrow 2NO(g)$ [2]
c) Using a catalytic converter. [1]
d) $2CO(g) + 2NO(g) \rightarrow 2CO_2(g) + N_2(g)$ [2]
e) Carbon dioxide [1]
9. **S** $6CO_2(g) + 6H_2O(l) \rightarrow C_6H_{12}O_6(s) + 6O_2(g)$ [2]

Page 110 Fuels
1. B [1]
2. B [1]
3. a) Fractional distillation [1]
b) [4]

Component	Chain length / number of carbon atoms per molecule	Volatility / ease of forming a vapour	Boiling point	Viscosity/ thickness of the liquid
Gasoline		✓ [1]		
Fuel oil	✓ [1]		✓ [1]	✓ [1]

c)

Component	Use
Gasoline	Fuel used in cars [1]
Kerosene	Jet fuel [1]
Fuel oil	Home heating systems / ships [1]
Bitumen	Making roads [1]

Page 111 Alkanes

1. D [1]
2. A [1]
3. a) A compound containing only carbon and hydrogen atoms [1]; all the carbon to carbon bonds are single bonds. [1]
   b) a family of compounds with similar chemical properties due to the presence of the same functional group [1]
   c) C_3H_8 [1]
   d)
   H—C—C—C—H [1]
   e) i) propane + oxygen → carbon dioxide + water [1]
      ii) $C_3H_8(g) + 5O_2(g) \rightarrow 3CO_2(g) + 4H_2O(l)$ [2]
4.

Butane [1]	2-methylpropane [1]

5. **S** a) In a substitution reaction one atom or group of atoms is replaced by another atom or group of atoms.
   b) In the presence of ultraviolet light. [1]
   c) $C_2H_6 + Cl_2 \rightarrow C_2H_5Cl + HCl$ [2]

Page 112 Alkenes

1. B [1]
2. a)
   C=C [1]
   b) An unsaturated hydrocarbon contains only hydrogen and carbon atoms [1]; and contains a C=C double bond. [1]
   c) i) Reaction with bromine / aqueous bromine [1]
      ii) The bromine is decolourised. [1]
3. a) High temperature [1], a catalyst [1]
   b) Fractional distillation [1]
4. **S** a) Only one product is formed. [1]
   b) An acid catalyst [1]
   c) $C_3H_6 + H_2O \rightarrow C_3H_7OH$ [2]
   d)
   H—C—C—C—OH [1]
5. **S** a) Compounds with the same molecular formulae but different structural formulae. [1]

b)

But-1-ene [1]	But-2-ene [1]

Page 113 Alcohols

1. C [1]
2.

Manufacturing method	Conditions needed	
	Temperature	One more condition
Fermentation of aqueous glucose	25–35 °C [1]	Presence of yeast [1] **or** Absence of oxygen [1]
Addition reaction between steam and ethene	300 °C [1]	High pressure / 6000 kPa / 60 atm [1] **or** Acid catalyst [1]

3. A solvent / a fuel [1]
4. a) ethanol + oxygen → carbon dioxide + water [1];
   $C_2H_5OH + 3O_2 \rightarrow 2CO_2 + 3H_2O$ [2]
   b) Carbon / carbon monoxide [1]
5. **S**

Manufacturing method	Advantages and disadvantages	
	Advantages	Disadvantages
Fermentation of aqueous glucose	Uses renewable resources / low energy consumption [1]	Slow process / yeast becomes less active as ethanol produced [1]
Addition reaction between steam and ethene	A quick process [1]	High costs / high energy consumption [1]

Page 114 Carboxylic acids

1. A [1]
2. D [1]
3. a)
   H—C—C [1]
   b) Carbon dioxide [1]
   c) ethanoic acid + sodium carbonate → sodium ethanoate + carbon dioxide + water [2]
   d) $2CH_3COOH + Na_2CO_3 \rightarrow 2CH_3COONa + CO_2 + H_2O$ [2]
4. **S** A [1]
5. a) **S** An ester [1]
   b) ethanoic acid + ethanol → ethyl ethanoate + water [1]
   c)
   H—C—C—O—C—C—H [2]
   d) $CH_3COOH + C_2H_5OH \rightarrow CH_3COOC_2H_5 + H_2O$ [2]
   e) An acid catalyst [1]
6. **S** a) Oxidation [1]
   b) Potassium manganate(VII) [1]

Page 115 Polymers

1. C [1]
2. a)
   C=C [1]

b)

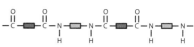
—C—C—C—C—C—C— [1]

c) Any **two** of: it cannot be converted back into ethene and repolymerised [1]; it cannot be recycled [1]; it takes a long time to break down. [1]
d) PET [1]
3. **S** a) A condensation polymer is made from two (or more) different monomers. [1]
   b) Nylon is a polyamide. [1]
   c)

   H—O—C—■—C—O—H

   A dicarboxylic acid [2]

   H—N—■—N—H

   A diamine [2]
   d)

   [2]
4. **S** a) Polyamide [1]
   b) Condensation polymer [1]
   c)
   [2]
   d)
   [2]

Pages 116-123: Section 12 Revise Questions

Page 117 Experimental design Quick Test

1. Accurate sketches of: **a)** gas syringe; **b)** burette or volumetric pipette.
2. X residue; Y filtrate
3. A saturated solution

Page 119 Acid-base titrations Quick Test

1. Burette
2. Pipette
3. Sucking the dilute alkali is dangerous as it could go into the mouth.
4. It is difficult to know how close the end-point is on the first titration.

Page 121 Chromatography, separation and purification Quick Test

1. A pure substance will show a single spot on the chromatogram. An impure substance will show more than one spot.
2. Filtration

Page 123 Identification of ions and gases Quick Test

1. Add dilute nitric acid and barium nitrate to the solution. A white precipitate indicates the presence of the sulfate ion.
2. Add aqueous sodium hydroxide to solutions of each ion. A green precipitate forms with the Fe^{2+} solution. A reddish-brown precipitate forms with the Fe^{3+} solution.
3. Light purple

Pages 124-127: Section 12 Practise Questions

Page 124 Experimental design
1. B [1]
2. B [1]
3. A [1]
4. a) Gas syringe [1]
   b) Balance [1]
   c) Measuring cylinder / burette [1]
   d) Thermometer [1]
   e) magnesium + hydrochloric acid →
      magnesium chloride + hydrogen [1]
   f) $Mg(s) + 2HCl(aq) \rightarrow MgCl_2(aq) + H_2(g)$
      [2]

Page 124 Acid–base titrations
1. a) Pipette [1]
   b) Burette [1]
   c) Methyl orange or thymolphthalein [1]
   d) Conical flask [1]
   e) To see the colour change of the
      indicator clearly. [1]
   f) Methyl orange – yellow to red;
      thymolphthalein – blue to colourless. [1]
   g) It is hard to know when the end-point is.
      [1] The indicator changes colour on the
      addition of one drop of acid. [1]
   h)

Titration	Initial volume of acid (cm³)	Final volume of acid (cm³)	Volume of acid added (cm³)
Trial	0.0	18.5 [1]	18.5
1st accurate	18.5	35.8	17.3 [1]
2nd accurate	0.0	17.4 [1]	17.4

   i) The two accurate results agree to within
      0.1 cm³. [1]
   j) sodium hydroxide + hydrochloric acid →
      sodium chloride + water [1]
   k) $NaOH(aq) + HCl(aq) \rightarrow NaCl(aq) + H_2O(l)$ [2]

Page 125 Chromatography, separation and purification
1.

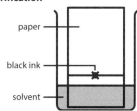

2. a) Impure [1]; it contains (at least) three
      components. [1]
   b) The solvent will not dissolve a pencil
      line. [1]
   c) The ink may have contained a dye(s)
      that reaches the top of the filter paper.
      [1]
   d) A [1]
   e) **S** 3 cm, 10 cm [1]; R_f = 0.3 [1]
3. **S** Use a locating agent [1], which can be
   sprayed onto the chromatogram. [1]
4. a) Lower boiling point [1]
   b) The fractional distillation of crude oil. [1]
5. a) A solid and a liquid [1]
   b) Any insoluble solid with any liquid [1]
6. A saturated solution [1]

7. a)

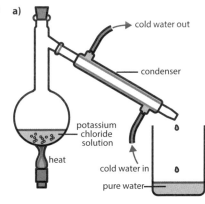

   Suitable container/flask for the potassium
   chloride solution [1]; condenser [1]; correct
   water flow through the condenser [1];
   suitable beaker / conical flask for collecting
   the water [1]
   b) Measure the melting or boiling point. [1]

Page 126 Identification of ions and gases
1. B [1]
2. D [1]
3. D [1]
4. Dip the nichrome wire in concentrated
   hydrochloric acid. [1]
   Dip the nichrome wire into the solid to be
   tested. [1]
   Put the nichrome wire into a blue Bunsen
   burner flame. [1]
5.

ion	Test	Result of test
Cu^{2+}	Flame test [1]	Blue–green colour [1]
CO_3^{2-}	Add dilute hydrochloric acid [1]	Carbon dioxide turns limewater cloudy [1]

6. a) White [1]
   b)

Ions	Test	Result
Sodium ion, Na^+	Flame test [1]	Yellow/orange colour [1]
Sulfate ion, SO_4^{2-}	Add dilute nitric acid and aqueous barium nitrate [1]	White precipitate [1]

7.

Gas	Test	Result
Chlorine	Damp litmus paper [1]	Litmus paper bleached [1]
Ammonia [1]	Damp red litmus paper	Litmus paper turns blue
Sulfur dioxide [1]	Acidified potassium manganate(VII)	Colour changes from purple to colourless [1]

8. a) Aqueous ammonia [1]
   b) A cation is a positively charged ion. [1]
   c)

Cation	Colour of precipitate
Fe^{2+} (iron(II) chloride)	Green [1]
Fe^{3+} [1]	Reddish brown [1]
Cr^{3+} [1]	Green (which dissolves in excess sodium hydroxide solution)
Al^{3+} (aluminium chloride)	White [1]

   d) iron(II) chloride + sodium hydroxide →
      iron(II) hydroxide + sodium chloride [1]
   e) $FeCl_2(aq) + 2NaOH(aq) \rightarrow Fe(OH)_2(s) + 2NaCl(aq)$ [2]
9. Add warm sodium hydroxide solution [1];
   damp indicator paper turns blue. [1]

Pages 128–139: Mixed Exam-Style Questions

1. a)

Element	Proton number	Electron number	Electronic configuration
Potassium	19 [1]	19	2,8,8,1 [1]
Oxygen	8	8 [1]	2,6 [1]

   b)

   [3]

2. a) Reversible reaction [1]
   b) i) Hydrated (copper(II) sulfate) [1]
      ii) It doesn't contain water [1]
   c) White [1]
   d) It is not a redox reaction [1]; there is no
      oxidation/reduction / no changes in
      oxidation states. [1]
3. a) Any **two** of: high densities; high melting
      points; form coloured compounds; often
      act as catalysts. [2]
   b) $4Fe + 3O_2 \rightarrow 2Fe_2O_3$ [2]
   c) i) $Fe_2O_3 + 3Mg \rightarrow 2Fe + 3MgO$ [2]
      ii) Iron(III) oxide [1]
      iii) Iron(III) oxide [1]
   d) Coke/carbon [1]; limestone [1]
4. a) **S** i) It is fully dissociated into ions. [1]
      ii) $HCl(aq) \rightarrow H^+(aq) + Cl^-(aq)$ [2]
      iii) $CH_3COOH(aq) \rightleftharpoons CH_3COO^-(aq) + H^+(aq)$ [2]
   b) i) A burette [1]
      ii) A pipette [1]
      iii)

Step 1: Write the equation.	$HCl + NaOH \rightarrow NaCl + H_2O$ [1]
Step 2: Write down the number of moles of the reactants.	$HCl + NaOH$ 1 mole 1 mole [1]
Step 3: Convert the moles into volumes and concentrations.	$HCl + NaOH$ 1000 cm³ 1000 cm³ 1M 1M [1]
Step 4: Use the same scaling factor for acid and alkali. The alkali is less concentrated than 0.1M as a greater volume was needed. So the scaling factor is 20/25 × 0.1.	$HCl + NaOH$ 1000 cm³ 0.1M + 1000 cm³ 0.1M [1] 20 cm³ 0.1M + 20/25 × 0.1M = 0.08M [1]

5. a) CH_3COOH [1]
   b) Ethanoic acid [1]
   c) i) Effervescence/ bubbling/ fizzing [1]
      ii) Carbon dioxide [1]
      iii) Use limewater [1]; limewater goes
         cloudy [1]
6. **S** a) Ethane = 30 [1]; ethene = 28 [1]
   b) i) Ethene [1]
      ii) As the particles have less mass they
         will move faster. [1]
   c) i) Ethane [1]
      ii) $C_2H_6 + Cl_2 \rightarrow C_2H_5Cl + HCl$ [2]

iii) Ultraviolet light [1]

7. a) So the ions are free to move. [1]
 b) i) Cathode [1]
 ii) Cations [1]
 iii) A substance that allows electric current to pass through it when it is molten or dissolved in water. [1]
 c) i) 7 [1]
 ii) Br^- [1]
 iii) Bromine [1]
 d) i) Displacement reaction [1]
 ii) Chlorine [1]; it displaces iodine from the sodium iodide. [1]

8. a) **S** Reduction [1]
 b) i) Calcium [1]
 ii) Copper [1]
 iii) It has a coating of oxide that reduces contact with other chemicals / acts as a barrier. [1]

9. **S** **a)** Exothermic [1]
 b) [2]

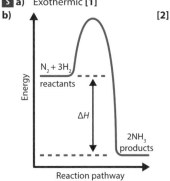

 c) i) To ensure a good rate of reaction [1]; even though a high temperature does not drive the equilibrium to the right / to the ammonia. [1]
 ii) A high pressure increases the proportion of ammonia [1]; in the equilibrium / drives the equilibrium position to the right. [1]
 iii) A catalyst increases the rate of reaction [1]; by reducing the activation energy of the reaction. [1]

10. a) $2Na(s) + 2H_2O(l) \rightarrow 2NaOH(aq) + H_2(g)$ [2]
 b) i) Use a burning splint. [1]
 ii) It burns with a 'pop'. [1]
 c) Alkali [1]
 d) Yellow [1]
 e) Neutralisation reaction [1]
 f) $H^+ + OH^- \rightarrow H_2O$ [1]

11. a)

Nitrogen (%)	Oxygen (%)	Carbon dioxide and noble gases (%)
78 [1]	21 [1]	1

 b) Noble gas atoms have full outer electron shells. [1]
 c) i) Burning of fossil fuels [1]
 ii) Increasing levels of carbon dioxide causes climate change / global warming. [1]
 iii) Photosynthesis [1]
 iv) Planting trees [1]

12. a) **S**

Step 1: Write the equation	$Zn + 2HNO_3 \rightarrow Zn(NO_3)_2 + H_2$
Step 2: Write down the number of moles of zinc and hydrogen.	1 mole → 1 mole [1]
Step 3: Convert the moles into mass and gaseous volume.	65 g → 24 dm^3 [1]
Step 4: Use the scaling factor.	$\frac{1.3}{65} \rightarrow 24 \times \frac{1.3}{65} = 0.48\ dm^3$ [2]

 b) $0.36/0.48 \times 100$ [1]; = 75% [1]

13. a)

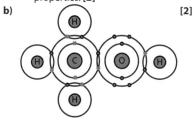
gas syringe [3]
dilute sulfuric acid
magnesium

 b) The mass of magnesium used [1]; the volume/concentration of dilute sulfuric acid. [1]
 c) i) An increase in temperature increased the rate of the reaction. [1]
 ii) At the start of the reaction. [1] When the concentration of the reactants is at its greatest / maximum collisions between reactants. [1]

14. **S** **a)** Any **two** from: having the same functional group; having the same general formula; differing from one member to the next by a $-CH_2-$ unit; displaying a trend in physical properties; sharing similar chemical properties. [2]
 b) [2]

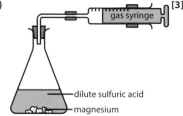

 c)

1. Write the equation	$2CH_3OH + 3O_2 \rightarrow 2CO_2 + 4H_2O$
2. Work out the energy needed to break the bonds. $\Delta H = +ve$	6 C–H = 2478 2 C–O = 716 2 O–H = 928 3 O=O = 1494 Total = +5616 [2]
3. Work out the energy released on forming the bonds. $\Delta H = -ve$	4 C=O = 2980 8 O–H = 3712 Total = −6692 [2]

4. Add the two energy changes together to get ΔH for the reaction.	+ 5616 − 6692 $\Delta H = - 1076$ kJ/mol [1]

 d)

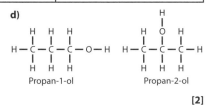

Propan-1-ol   Propan-2-ol [2]

15. a) i) Melting [1]
 ii) Condensation [1]
 b) The particles move closer together / the gas could condense to a liquid. [1]
 c) i) The atoms are held together by strong bonds forming a very strong structure. [1]
 ii) Graphite has delocalised electrons which can move along the layers of atoms. [1]
 d) i) Any one of: chromium; nickel; carbon. [1]
 ii) Its hardness [1]; and resistance to corrosion. [1]

16. a)

Metal	Reaction with dilute hydrochloric acid. Use ✓ for a reaction and ✗ for no reaction
Iron	✓ [1]
Copper	✗ [1]
Zinc	✓ [1]

 b) $Mg(s) + H_2O(g) \rightarrow MgO(s) + H_2(g)$ [2]
 c) i) $C(s) + 2PbO(s) \rightarrow CO_2(g) + 2Pb(s)$ [2]
 ii) Carbon [1]
 iii) Aluminium / any metal above carbon in the reactivity series. [1]

17. **S** **a)** Condensation polymer [1]
 b) It can be converted back into monomers and re-polymerised / it is recyclable. [1]
 c) i)

(diagram of monomers with C=C bonds) [2]

 ii) Addition polymer [1]
 d)

Gas	Environmental problem
Carbon monoxide	A toxic gas / damaging to health [1]
Carbon dioxide	Increase global warming / climate change [1]

18. a) A hydrocarbon is a compound that contains hydrogen and carbon only. [1]
 b) A homologous series is a family of similar compounds with similar chemical properties [1]; due to the presence of the same functional group. [1]

c)

Characteristic	Alkane or alkene?
An unsaturated hydrocarbon	Alkene **[1]**
General formula C_nH_{2n+2}	Alkane **[1]**
Undergoes a substitution reaction with chlorine	Alkane **[1]**
Manufactured in a process called cracking	Alkene **[1]**
Decolourises aqueous bromine	Alkene **[1]**

d) i) Fractional distillation **[1]**
   ii) Road building **[1]**

19. S a)

Relative atomic mass from ^{24}Mg	$24 \times 79/100 = 18.96$ **[1]**
Relative atomic mass from ^{25}Mg	$25 \times 10/100 = 2.50$ **[1]**
Relative atomic mass from ^{26}Mg	$26 \times 11/100 = 2.86$ **[1]**
Total relative atomic mass (3 significant figures)	24.3 **[1]**

b) A pure metal has only one type of atom. The rows of these atoms can slide over each other. **[1]** In an alloy the different sized atoms means the layers of atoms cannot slide over each other. **[1]**

c) i) Galvanising **[1]**
   ii) The zinc is more reactive than iron **[1]**; the zinc reacts in preference to the iron by losing electrons. **[1]**

20. a) S

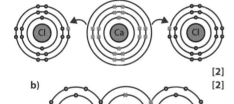

[2]

b) **[2]**

c) i) Strong electrostatic forces between the ions. **[1]**
   ii) When molten or dissolved in water the ions are free to move. **[1]**

d) It has weak intermolecular forces between its molecules. **[1]**

e) $2NaOH + CaCl_2 \rightarrow Ca(OH)_2 + 2NaCl$ **[2]**

21. S a) Any three from: concentration of dilute hydrochloric acid; volume of hydrochloric acid; temperature of hydrochloric acid; mass of marble chips. **[3]**

b) The smaller the size of the chips, the greater the surface area and therefore the greater the rate of the reaction. **[1]** There will be more collisions between the particles of the marble chips and the hydrochloric acid particles. **[1]**

c) i) 10–20 seconds **[1]**
   ii)

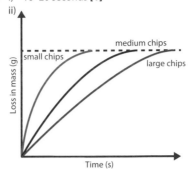

[3]

Pages 140-151: Practice Paper 1 (1 mark each)

1	C	21	B
2	B	22	B
3	B	23	B
4	B	24	A
5	B	25	D
6	D	26	C
7	D	27	D
8	B	28	B
9	A	29	D
10	C	30	B
11	A	31	C
12	C	32	C
13	A	33	A
14	D	34	B
15	A	35	D
16	C	36	A
17	D	37	B
18	B	38	D
19	C	39	C
20	A	40	B

Pages 152-163: Practice Paper 2 (1 mark each)

1	C	21	C
2	D	22	D
3	D	23	B
4	B	24	B
5	B	25	D
6	B	26	C
7	C	27	C
8	B	28	A
9	D	29	C
10	D	30	D
11	C	31	A
12	C	32	C
13	C	33	C
14	C	34	D
15	C	35	C
16	B	36	C
17	A	37	D
18	B	38	B
19	D	39	A
20	C	40	A

Pages 164-171: Practice Paper 3

1. a)

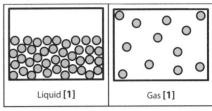

Liquid **[1]**   Gas **[1]**

[2]

b) i) Boiling/evaporation **[1]**
   ii) Condensation **[1]**

c) The speed of movement of particles in a gas is greater than in a liquid. **[1]**

2. a)

Type of particle	Relative mass	Relative charge
Proton	1	+1 **[1]**
Neutron	1 **[1]**	0
Electron	1/2000	−1 **[1]**

b) i) 11 **[1]**
   ii) 12 **[1]**
   iii) 2,8,1 **[1]**
   iv) 2,8 **[1]**

3. a) **[2]**

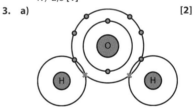

b) No ions (to carry the charge) **[1]**; no electrons free to move **[1]**

4. a) calcium + oxygen → calcium oxide **[1]**

b) $2Ca(s) + O_2(g) \rightarrow 2CaO(s)$ **[2]**

c) i) Base **[1]**
   ii) Salt **[1]**

d) 56 **[1]**

5. a)

Electrolyte	Product at the anode	Product at the cathode
Molten lead (ii) bromide	Bromine	Lead **[1]**
Dilute sulfuric acid	Oxygen **[1]**	Hydrogen
Molten aluminium oxide	Oxygen **[1]**	Aluminium

b) Carbon/graphite or platinum **[1]**

c) Improve appearance / prevent corrosion **[1]**

6. a) The temperature of the surroundings will decrease. **[1]**

b) An endothermic reaction **[1]**

7. a) Gas syringe **[1]**

b) i) Any **two** of: the mass of calcium carbonate; the volume of acid; the temperature of the acid. **[2]**
   ii) The concentration of the acid **[1]**

197

c) i)

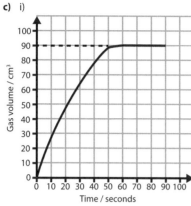

[2]

ii) The rate of the reaction is greatest at the beginning [1]; this is when the concentration of the acid is at its greatest. [1]

8. a) +2 [1]
   b) Magnesium [1]
   c) Redox [1]
9. a) Y [1]
   b) X [1]
   c) Red [1]
   d) $H^+(aq) + OH^-(aq) \rightarrow H_2O(l)$ [2]
10. a) Stage 1: Put the acid in a beaker / suitable container and add the copper (II) carbonate. [1]
    Stage 2: Stir the mixture. [1]
    Stage 3: Filter to remove excess solid. [1]
    Stage 4: Evaporate the solution in an evaporating dish. [1]
    Stage 5: Leave the solution to crystallise. [1]
    b) Hydrated [1]
11. a) i) The elements are in the same group of the Periodic Table (Group I). [1]
       ii) The elements all have one electron in their outer electron shell. [1]
    b) 1+ / +1/ K^+ [1]
    c) Potassium [1]
    d) i) Use nichrome wire [1]; dip wire into concentrated hydrochloric acid then the solid, then the flame. [1]
       ii) Lilac / light purple [1]
12. a) They exist as single/uncombined atoms. [1]
    b) Inert means they are unreactive. [1] Noble gases have complete outer electron shells. [1]
13. a) Calcium [1]
    b) Copper [1]
    c) i) magnesium + steam → magnesium oxide + hydrogen [1]
       ii) $Mg(s) + H_2O(g) \rightarrow MgO(s) + H_2(g)$ [2]
    d) Any **two** of: painting; greasing; coating with plastic; galvanising. [2]
14. a) Fertilisers [1]
    b) Fertilisers / detergents [1]
    c) Deoxygenation of water / damage to aquatic life [1]
15. a) A compound containing only hydrogen and carbon. [1]
    b) Fractional distillation [1]
    c) i) Methane [1]
       ii) [1]

H—C—H with H top and H bottom

d) i)

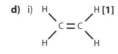

[1]

ii) Cracking [1]
iii)

Test	Result for unsaturated hydrocarbon
Aqueous bromine [1]	Bromine decolorised [1]

iv) An addition polymer [1]

Pages 172-178: Practice Paper 4

1.

Change made to a gas	Effect on the volume of the gas	Explanation for the change using kinetic particle theory
Increase in temperature	Increase [1]	The particles gain energy and move faster reducing the attractions between the particles. [1]
Increase in pressure	Decrease [1]	The particles move closer together, their movement decreases and the attractions between the particles increase. [1]

b)

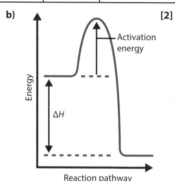

[2]

c) Exothermic [1]
d) $2Na(s) + 2H_2O(l) \rightarrow 2NaOH(aq) + H_2(g)$ [2]

2. a) 2,8,3 [1]
   b) Al^{3+} [1]
   c) i) Al_2O_3 [1]
      ii) 102 [1]
      iii) 10.2 g [1]
      iv) $4Al(s) + 3O_2(g) \rightarrow 2Al_2O_3(s)$ [2]
   d)

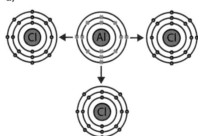

[2]

   e) i) Aluminium oxide [1]
      ii) To lower the melting point [1]
      iii) They react with oxygen, forming carbon dioxide. [1]
      iv) $Al^{3+} + 3e^- \rightarrow Al$ [2]

3. a) Any two of: same functional group; same general formula; each member differs from the next by $-CH_2-$; displaying a trend in physical properties; sharing similar chemical properties. [2]

b)

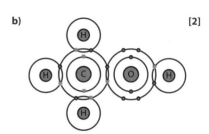

[2]

c) The forces between the molecules are weak / weak intermolecular forces. [1]
d) $2CH_3OH + 3O_2 \rightarrow 2CO_2 + 4H_2O$ [2]
e)

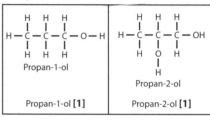

Propan-1-ol [1]   Propan-2-ol [1]

4. a) Na^+, Br^-, H^+, OH^- [2]
   b) $4OH^- \rightarrow 2H_2O + O_2 + 4e^-$ [2]
   c) $2H^+ + 2e^- \rightarrow H_2$ [2]
   d) Bromine would be formed. [1]
5. a) The rate of the forward reaction equals the rate of the backwards reaction / the concentrations of reactants and products are no longer changing. [1]
   b) i) Iron [1]
      ii) It lowers/reduces the activation energy. [1]
      iii) Damp red litmus paper turns blue. [1]
   c) i) Methane [1]; carbon dioxide [1]
      ii) The absorption/reflection of thermal energy [1]; reducing the loss of thermal energy to space. [1]
   d) Temperatures in a car engine are high and in these conditions, nitrogen in the air can react with oxygen, forming nitrogen oxides. [1]
6. a) A base that is soluble in water and in aqueous solution produces OH^- ions. [1]
   b) $CuSO_4(aq) + 2NaOH(aq) \rightarrow Cu(OH)_2(s) + Na_2SO_4(aq)$ [2]
   c) $64 + (16 \times 2) + (1 \times 2) = 98$ g [1]
   d) $50/1000 \times 0.1 = 0.005$ moles [1]
   e) 2 moles NaOH → 1 mole $Cu(OH)_2$
      0.005 moles → 0.0025 moles
      0.005 moles → $0.0025 \times 98 = 0.245$ g [3]
   f) $0.2/0.245 = 81.6\%$ (82%) [2]
7. a)

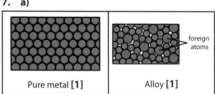

   Pure metal [1]   Alloy [1]

   b) In the pure metal the rows of atoms can slide and move their position [1]; in the alloy the additional atoms stop the rows of metal atoms from sliding. [1]
   c) i) +II (+2) [1]
      ii) 2+ [1]
      iii) X [1]
   d) The zinc is more reactive than iron [1]; the zinc reacts with oxygen/water and so limits the same reaction for iron. [1]
8. a) $C_nH_{2n+1}COOH$ [1]

b) 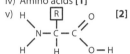 **[2]**

c) i) Acid (catalyst) **[1]**
   ii) Esters **[1]**
   iii) **[2]**

$$H-\overset{\overset{\displaystyle H}{|}}{\underset{\underset{\displaystyle H}{|}}{C}}-\overset{\overset{\displaystyle O}{\|}}{C}-O-\overset{\overset{\displaystyle H}{|}}{\underset{\underset{\displaystyle H}{|}}{C}}-\overset{\overset{\displaystyle H}{|}}{\underset{\underset{\displaystyle H}{|}}{C}}-H$$

d) i) Condensation polymer **[1]**
   ii) Amine **[1]**
   iii) Polyamides **[1]**
   iv) Amino acids **[1]**
   v) **[2]**

$$\overset{\overset{\displaystyle H}{|}}{\underset{\underset{\displaystyle H}{|}}{N}}-\overset{\overset{\displaystyle R}{|}}{\underset{\underset{\displaystyle H}{|}}{C}}-\overset{\overset{\displaystyle O}{\|}}{C}\overset{}{\underset{\underset{\displaystyle O-H}{}}{}}$$

Pages 180-185: Practice Paper 6

1. a) i) Some of the zinc carbonate remained unreacted / no further effervescence. **[1]**
   ii) Filtration **[1]**
   iii) Filtrate **[1]**
   iv) Transfer the solution/filtrate to an evaporating dish **[1]**; heat the solution until saturated / crystals form on cooling **[1]**; leave the solution to cool and crystallise **[1]**; dry the crystals with filter paper. **[1]**

b)

Ions formed when zinc chloride crystals dissolve in distilled water	Test used	Results confirming the identification
Zinc ions	Add aqueous sodium hydroxide.	White precipitate forms which dissolves in excess sodium hydroxide giving a colourless solution. **[1]**
Chloride ions	Add dilute nitric acid and silver nitrate solution. **[1]**	White precipitate forms. **[1]**

2. a) The metal can is a better conductor of thermal energy than glass / will ensure more thermal energy is transferred to the water. **[1]**

b) The same volume of water in the metal can. **[1]**

c)

Fuel	Rise in temperature of the water (°C)	Mass of spirit burner and fuel before burning (g)	Mass of spirit burner and fuel after burning (g)	Mass of fuel burnt (g)	Temperature rise per 1 g of fuel burnt (°C/g)
X	28	42.6	41.2	1.4 **[1]**	20.0 **[1]**
Y	25	40.2	39.3	0.9 **[1]**	27.8
Z	27	44.3	42.8 **[1]**	1.5	18.0 **[1]**

d) Y **[1]**

3. a) It is easier to add / easier to use the same mass (measure length). **[1]**

b) i) The one taken after 30 seconds. **[1]**
   ii)

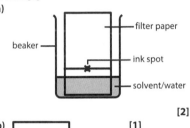

Correctly labelled axes with units **[1]**; points correctly plotted **[1]**; smooth curve drawn. **[1]**

   iii) Any **one** of: the same mass/length of magnesium ribbon; the same volume of the dilute nitric acid. **[1]**
   iv) The rate of reaction will be lower/smaller. **[1]**
   v) See second line in diagram in ii) above. **[2]**

4. a) Carbon/graphite or platinum **[1]**

b) i) Anode **[1]**
   ii) Oxygen **[1]**
   iii) A glowing splint relights. **[1]**
   iv) Hydrogen **[1]**
   v) 'Pops' with a lighted splint. **[1]**

5. P is chromium nitrate **[2]**; Q is sodium iodide. **[2]**

6. a)

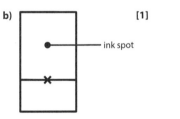

[2]

b) **[1]**

ink spot

ink spot

F

Filtration   the liquid or solution that has passed through a filter   121

Formula   a mixture that has been carefully designed to have specific properties   22

Fossil fuel   a fuel made from the remains of decayed animal and plant matter compressed over millions of years   96

Fractional distillation   a process for separating liquids with different boiling points   96, 121

Freezing   changing a liquid to a solid   6

Fuel cell   a cell that produces electricity from the chemical energy of a fuel. A hydrogen–oxygen fuel cell uses hydrogen and oxygen to produce electricity   43

Functional group   an atom or group of atoms that determine the chemical properties of a homologous series   100, 102

G

Galvanising   the process of coating a metal (usually iron) with zinc   80

Gases   the state of matter in which the substance has no set volume or shape   6

Giant covalent structure   a structure made of very many atoms joined together by covalent bonds   18

Giant lattice structure   ionic crystal   15

Greenhouse gases   a gas that can trap long-wave radiation emitted from the Earth's surface   95

Group   a vertical column of elements in the Periodic Table   11

H

Haber process   the process in which ammonia is manufactured from nitrogen and hydrogen   48, 72

Haematite   a mineral form of iron (iii) oxide   81

Heating curves   a plot of temperature versus time that represents the phase changes that a substance undergoes as heat is continuously added at a constant rate   7

Homologous series   a group of organic compounds with the same general formula, similar chemical properties and physical properties that change gradually from one member of the series to the next   98, 100, 102

Hydrated   a substance that is chemically combined with water   48, 55

Hydrocarbon   a compound containing hydrogen and carbon only   96

I

Indicator   a substance that changes colour in either an acid or an alkali and so can be used to identify acids or alkalis.   52

Insoluble salt   does not dissolve in water   55

Intermolecular   the force of attraction or repulsion between molecules   17

Ionic equation   a chemical equation showing how the ions involved react together   23, 53

Ions   charged atoms or molecules   12

Isotope   different atoms of the same element that have the same number of protons but different numbers of neutrons   12

K

Kinetic particle theory   the theory describing the movement of particles in solids, liquids and gases   6, 8

L

Liquid   the state of matter in which a substance has a fixed volume but no definite shape   6

Locating agent   a substance used to show the position of a colourless product on a chromatogram   120

Lubricant   a substance that helps to reduce friction between surfaces in mutual contact, which ultimately reduces the heat generated when the surfaces move   18

M

Malleable   can be hammered into shape   20

Mass number (nucleon number)   the number of protons and neutrons in an atom (also known as the nucleon number)   10

Melting   changing a solid into a liquid at its melting point   6

Mixture   two or more substances combined without a chemical reaction – they can be separated easily   10

Molar gas volume   the volume of one mole of a gas at r.t.p.   26

Mole   the amount of a substance containing 6.02×10^{23} particles (atoms, molecules, ions)   26

Molecular formula   the number and type of different atoms in one molecule   22, 27

Monatomic   an element composed of separate atoms   73

Monomer   small molecules that can be joined in a chain to make a polymer   106

N

Neutralisation reaction   a reaction in which an acid reacts with a base or alkali to form a salt and water   53

Neutron   sub-atomic particle in the nucleus of atoms that has mass but no charge   12

Nichrome wire   a family of alloys of nickel and chromium (and occasionally iron) commonly used as resistance wire   123

Nucleon number   see **mass number**

Nucleus   the tiny centre of an atom, typically made up of protons and neutrons   10

O

Oxidation   the gain of oxygen, loss of electrons or increase in oxidation number   50

Oxidation number   the degree of oxidation of an element   72

Oxidising agent   a substance that will oxidise another substance   50

P

Percentage yield   the proportion of the actual amount of product formed in a chemical reaction, compared to the expected amount as predicted by the equation   27

Period   a row in the Periodic Table, from an alkali metal to a noble gas   11

Periodic Table   the modern arrangement of the chemical elements in groups and periods   10, 11

pH scale   a scale measuring the acidity (lower than 7) or alkalinity of a solution (higher than 7). It is a measure of the concentration of hydrogen ions in a solution   52

Photosynthesis   the reaction between carbon dioxide and water to produce glucose in the presence of chlorophyll and using energy from light   95

Physical change   a change in a substance that is easily reversed and does not involve the making of new chemical bonds   46

Physical properties   characteristics of matter that can be observed and measured without changing the chemical identity of the sample   68, 70, 74

Pipette   a type of laboratory tool commonly used in chemistry and biology to transport a measured volume of liquid, often as a media dispenser   118

Polyamide   any polymer (substance composed of long, multiple-unit molecules) in which the repeating units in the molecular chain are linked   107

Polyester   a type of condensation polymer   107

Polymer   a large molecule built up from many smaller molecules called monomers

Precipitate   a reaction in which an insoluble salt is formed by mixing two solutions   122

Proton   positively charged sub-atomic particles in the nucleus of atoms   10

Proton number   see **atomic number**

R

Reacting masses   a mass against which a system operates in order to produce acceleration   24

Reaction pathway diagram   shows the energies of the reactants, the transition state(s) and the products of the reaction with time   45

Reactivity series   a list of elements showing their relative reactivities. More reactive elements will displace less reactive ones from their compounds   75, 78

Recycling   a process in which new items are. made from products that have been used before   106

Redox reactions   a reaction involving simultaneous reduction and oxidation   50

Reducing agent   a substance that will reduce another substance   50

Published by Collins
An imprint of HarperCollins*Publishers*
The News Building, 1 London Bridge Street, London, SE1 9GF, UK

HarperCollins*Publishers*
Macken House, 39/40 Mayor Street Upper, Dublin 1, D01 C9W8, Ireland

Browse the complete Collins catalogue at
collins.co.uk

© HarperCollins*Publishers* Limited 2024

10 9 8 7 6 5 4 3 2 1

ISBN 978-0-00-867090-0

British Library Cataloguing-in-Publication Data
A catalogue record for this publication is available from the British Library.

Author: **Chris Sunley**
Expert reviewer: **Dr Rahul Sharma**
Publisher: **Elaine Higgleton**
Product manager: **Jennifer Hall**
Editors: **Aidan Gill, David Hemsley**
Proofreaders and answer checkers: **Arlo Porter, Keith Gallick, Beth Hutchins**
Cover designer: **Gordon MacGilp**
Cover artwork: **Drawlab19/Shutterstock**
Internal designer and illustrator: **PDQ Media**
Typesetter: **PDQ Media**
Production controller: **Lyndsey Rogers**
Printed in India by Multivista Global Pvt. Ltd.

Acknowledgements
With thanks to the following teachers who provided feedback during the development stages: Shalini Reddy, Manthan International School; Dr Rahul Sharma, IRA Global School; Gauri Tendulkar, JBCN International School; Sejal Vasarkar, SVKM JV Parekh International School.

Cambridge International Education material in this publication is reproduced under licence and remains the intellectual property of Cambridge University Press & Assessment.

This text has not been through the endorsement process for the Cambridge Pathway. Any references or materials related to answers, grades, papers or examinations are based on the opinion of the author(s). The Cambridge International Education syllabus or curriculum framework associated assessment guidance material and specimen papers should always be referred to for definitive guidance.

Photographs
P 8 Dafinka/Shutterstock, p 69 IanRedding/Shutterstock, p 70 (l) Rvkamalov gmail.com/Shutterstock, p 70 (c) Rvkamalov gmail.com/ Shutterstock, p 70 (r) historiasperiodicas/ Shutterstock, p 73 Slaven/Shutterstock, p 118 Torychemistry/ Shutterstock

NOTES

NOTES

NOTES

NOTES

NOTES